STOKELY CARMICHAEL

The Story of Black Power

The History of the Civil Rights Movement

STOKELY CARMICHAEL

The Story of Black Power

by *Jacqueline Johnson*

With an Introduction by

ANDREW YOUNG

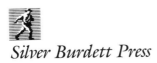

Silver Burdett Press

*This book is dedicated to the Jenkins and Johnson clan,
Jamila, Mytari, Chijoke, and the memory of Yusuf Hawkins.
Power to our generations!*

I would like to give special thanks to Kwame Ture, Elaine Carmichael, Mabel Carmichael, David Brothers, and Mari Jo Johnson for helping make this book more of what it should be. Also thanks to Doris Jean Austin, Della Rowland, Mark Davies, Duma Ndluvo, F. D. Reese, Rev. James Anderson, Brenda Connor Bey, the Pen American Center and the New York Foundation for the Arts, Gloria Johnson, Oke Sande, Maliaka Adero, Pat Warrington, Ted Lawton, Florence Hardne, Julie Broglin, New Renaissance Writers' Guild, Orisaiye, Olosumi, and Lawrence Jordan.

Series Consultant: Aldon Morris
Cover and Text Design: Design Five, New York
Maps: General Cartography, Inc.
Series Editorial Supervisor: Richard G. Gallin
Series Supervision of Art and Design: Leslie Bauman
Series Editing: Agincourt Press
Concept Editor: Della Rowland
Consultants: James Marion Gray, Ph.D., Teacher, Lincoln Park High School, Lincoln Park, Michigan; Fath Ruffins, Historian, National Museum of American History, Smithsonian Institution, Washington, D.C.

Published by Silver Burdett Press, Inc., a division of Simon & Schuster, Inc., Prentice Hall Building, Englewood Cliffs, NJ 07632.

Permissions and photo credits appear on page 130.

Library of Congress Cataloging-in-Publication Data

Johnson, Jacqueline.
   Stokely Carmichael: the story of black power / by Jacqueline Johnson; with an introduction by Andrew Young.
   p.   cm. —(The History of the civil rights movement)
   Includes bibliographical references and index.
   Summary: A biography of the man who made famous the words "Black Power" as he fought for the rights of black people in this country, and later settled in Africa where he organizes young Africans to work for their rights.
   1. Carmichael, Stokely—Juvenile literature.   2. Afro-Americans— Biography—Juvenile literature.   3. Civil rights workers—United States— Juvenile literature.   [1. Carmichael, Stokely.   2. Civil rights workers.
3. Blacks—Biography.]   I. Title.   II. Series.
E185.97.C27J58   1990
323′.092—dc20
[B]
[92]   90-31803
ISBN 0-382-09920-6 (lib. bdg.)   CIP
ISBN 0-382-24056-1 (pbk.)   AC

CONTENTS

INTRODUCTION
By Andrew Young

Some thirty years ago, a peaceful revolution took place in the United States, as African Americans sought equal rights. That revolution, which occurred between 1954 and 1968, is called the civil rights movement. Actually, African Americans have been struggling for their civil rights for as long as they have been in this country. Before the Civil War, brave abolitionists were calling out for an end to the injustice and cruelty of slavery. Even after the Civil War freed slaves, African Americans were still forced to fight other forms of racism and discrimination—segregation and prejudice. This movement still continues today as people of color battle racial hatred and economic exploitation all over the world.

The books in this series tell the stories of the lives of Ella Baker, Stokely Carmichael, Fannie Lou Hamer, Jesse Jackson, Malcolm X, Thurgood Marshall, Rosa Parks, A. Philip Randolph, and Martin Luther King, Jr.—just a few of the thousands of brave people who worked in the civil rights movement. Learning about these heroes is an important lesson in American history. They risked their homes and their jobs—and some gave their lives—to secure rights and freedoms that we now enjoy and often take for granted.

Most of us know the name of Dr. Martin Luther King, Jr., the nonviolent leader of the movement. But others who were just as important may not be as familiar. Rosa Parks insisted on her right to a seat on a public bus. Her action started a bus boycott that changed a segregation law and sparked a movement.

Ella Baker was instrumental in founding two major civil rights organizations, the Southern Christian Leadership Conference (SCLC) and the Student Nonviolent Coordinating Committee (SNCC). One of the chairpersons of SNCC, Stokely Carmichael, is perhaps best known for making the slogan "Black Power" famous. Malcolm X, the strong voice from the urban north, rose from a prison inmate to a powerful black Muslim leader.

Not many people know that the main organizer of the 1963 March on Washington was A. Philip Randolph. Younger leaders called Randolph the "father of the movement." Fannie Lou Hamer, a poor sharecropper from Mississippi, was such a powerful speaker for voters rights that President Lyndon Johnson blocked out television coverage of the 1964 Democratic National Convention to keep her off the air. Thurgood Marshall was the first African American to be made a Supreme Court justice.

Many who demanded equality paid for their actions. They were fired from their jobs, thrown out of their homes, beaten, and even killed. But they marched, went to jail, and put their lives on the line over and over again for the right to equal justice. These rights include something as simple as being able to sit and eat at a lunch counter. They include political rights such as the right to vote. They also include the equal rights to education and job opportunities that lead to economic betterment.

We are now approaching a level of democracy that allows all citizens of the United States to participate in the American dream. Jesse Jackson, for example, has pursued the dream of the highest office in this land, the president of the United States. Jackson's running for president was made possible by those who went before him. They are the people whose stories are included in this biography and history series, as well as thousands of others who remain nameless. They are people who depend upon you to carry on the dream of liberty and justice for all people of the world.

Civil Rights Movement Time Line

—1954————1955————1956————1957—

May 17—
Brown v. *Board of Education of Topeka I*: Supreme Court rules racial segregation in public is unconstitutional.

May 31—
Brown v. *Board of Education of Topeka II*: Supreme Court says desegregation of public schools must proceed "with all deliberate speed."

August 28—
14-year-old Emmett Till is killed in Money, Mississippi.

December 5, 1955–December 20, 1956—
Montgomery, Alabama bus boycott.

November 13—
Supreme Court outlaws racial segregation on Alabama's city buses.

January 10, 11—
Southern Christian Leadership Conference (SCLC) is founded.

August 29—
Civil Rights Act is passed. Among other things, it creates Civil Rights Commission to advise the president and gives government power to uphold voting rights.

September 1957–
Little Rock Central High School is desegregated.

—1962————1963————1964—

September 29—
Federal troops help integrate University of Mississippi ("Ole Miss") after two people are killed and several are injured.

April to May—
Birmingham, Alabama, demonstrations. School children join the marches.

May 20—
Supreme Court rules Birmingham's segregation laws are unconstitutional.

June 12—
NAACP worker Medgar Evers is killed in Jackson, Mississippi.

August 28—
March on Washington draws more than 250,000 people.

September 15—
Four girls are killed when a Birmingham church is bombed.

November 22—
President John F. Kennedy is killed in Dallas, Texas.

March–June—
St. Augustine, Florida, demonstrations.

June 21—
James Chaney, Michael Schwerner, and Andrew Goodman are killed while registering black voters in Mississippi.

July 2—
Civil Rights Act is passed. Among other things, it provides for equal job opportunities and gives the government power to sue to desegregate public schools and facilities.

August—
Mississippi Freedom Democratic Party (MFDP) attempts to represent Mississippi at the Democratic National Convention.

1958 — 1959 — 1960 — 1961

September 1958–August 1959—
Little Rock Central High School is closed because governor refuses to integrate it.

February 1—
Student sit-ins at lunch counter in Greensboro, North Carolina, begin sit-in protests all over the South.

April 17—
Student Nonviolent Coordinating Committee (SNCC) is founded.

May 6—
Civil Rights Act is passed. Among other things, it allows judges to appoint people to help blacks register to vote.

Eleven African countries win their independence.

May 4—
Freedom Rides leave Washington, D.C., and head south.

September 22—
Interstate Commerce Commission ordered to enforce desegregation laws on buses, and trains, and in travel facilities like waiting rooms, rest rooms, and restaurants.

1965 — 1966 — 1967 — 1968

January–March—
Selma, Alabama, demonstrations.

February 21—
Malcolm X is killed in New York City.

March 21–25—
More than 25,000 march from Selma to Montgomery, Alabama.

August 6—
Voting Rights Act passed.

August 11–16—
Watts riot (Los Angeles, California).

June—
James Meredith "March Against Fear" from Memphis, Tennessee, to Jackson, Mississippi. Stokely Carmichael makes slogan "Black Power" famous during march.

Fall—
Black Panther Party for Self-Defense is formed by Huey Newton and Bobby Seale in Oakland, California.

June 13—
Thurgood Marshall is appointed first African-American U.S. Supreme Court justice.

Summer—
Riots break out in 30 U.S. cities.

April 4—
Martin Luther King, Jr., is killed in Memphis, Tennessee.

April 11—
Civil Rights Act is passed. Among other things, it prohibits discrimination in selling and renting houses or apartments.

May 13–June 23—
Poor People's March: Washington, D.C., to protest poverty.

In order for a people to develop . . . they must hold a high regard for themselves. They must know that they came from *somewhere*, in order to believe themselves capable of going somewhere; they must have a past before they can create a future for themselves. A people needs legends, heroes, myths. Deny them these and you have won half the battle against them.

John Oliver Killens, *Black Man's Burden*

*To stoke something means to fuel
a fire, make a fire, to make a revolution.
Such is the life of Stokely Carmichael/Kwame Ture,
one who fuels the fire of revolution.*

1 LITTLE MAN OF TRINIDAD (FROM TRINIDAD TO AMERICA)

> ❝ *[I predict] that there will soon be a turning point in the West Indies...; and that the people who inhabit that portion of the Western hemisphere will be the instruments for uniting a scattered race.* ❞
>
> MARCUS GARVEY, a black leader who wanted to found a black homeland in Africa

On July 29, 1941, in Port of Spain, Trinidad, a boy was born. Twenty years later, in the United States he would raise his fist in a symbol that shocked the world. One day he would be famous for two words that fired up people around the world. Those words were "black power." His name was Stokely, son of Mabel and Adolphus Carmichael.

Trinidad, which is part of the West Indies, is a large island in the Caribbean Sea. It is about 1,500 miles from the United States and about the size of the state of Delaware. Port of Spain, the capital of Trinidad, is a seaport town. When Stokely was a boy, the town had a large black population and a growing number of Creoles. Creoles are people of mixed race.

During the 1940s, Trinidad was a poor country where most of the people made their living by farming sugarcane or cocoa beans. But many of them moved into the cities to try to find work in the factories and in government jobs. Trinidad was a crown colony of Great Britain. This meant that English whites had all the power in Trinidad, because Trinidad was ruled from London. All the laws were made there, and the English people in power often showed prejudice against the large black population of the island.

The whites thought that they were better than the blacks. But the blacks had a defense against the bad treatment they received from the whites. They put on a "thick skin"—they learned to ignore insults and to turn away from embarrassing moments. But this thick skin didn't prevent the blacks of Trinidad from relying on themselves and speaking up for themselves. They were politically active in government, law-enforcement agencies, and education. Still, the life-style of blacks and whites in Trinidad was separate and unequal.

The Carmichael family lived a comfortable life together. Stokely had good food to eat and nice clothes to wear. His father was a skilled carpenter, and he had built a big house for the family to live in at 54 Oxford Street. The Carmichaels also received money from Mabel Carmichael's parents, who lived in the United States.

As a small child, Stokely felt sympathy for other children who weren't as well off as he was. When he was about six, he often sneaked food out of the house and took it with him to school. There he gave it to friends he knew were hungry. If the grown-ups didn't watch him closely, he gave away his clothes, too. Stokely's grandmother finally had to hide his clothes and tell him to bring his friends home for lunch.

Stokely was a handsome little boy with big eyes and a flashing smile. He also had a sharp wit and a good mind. He loved to read. When he needed a break, he and his friends played a game of cricket—an English game that is very much like baseball.

Like other children in Trinidad, Stokely was often excited when carnival time came every year. It was usually in February

or March and took place just before the Roman Catholic observation of Lent. At carnival time, the people of Trinidad dressed up in costumes and had big celebrations, parades, and parties. These lasted for days at a time. There were steel bands and calypso music playing all over the island. Trinidad has one of the oldest carnival traditions in the Western Hemisphere. Stokely liked to sneak away from his aunts' watchful eyes and follow the parades and bands. He also took part in the "jump ups," or "Jourvets," that occurred. Jourvets were carnival celebrations that took place all night long.

At this time Stokely and three of his sisters were living with their two aunts and their grandmother. In 1944, soon after Stokely was born, Mabel Carmichael went to the United States to live with her parents. Stokely was three years old at this time. A year later, Adolphus Carmichael left Trinidad to join his wife in the United States.

Before she left Trinidad, Mabel Carmichael placed Stokely in a private school. In Trinidad, it was a common practice to put children into school by the time they were three years old. The school was called the Eastern Boys Government School. Stokely was known as "little man" among the family's neighbors and friends. He got this name because he often acted wise beyond his years. For example, he was very aware of what went on in local politics.

During the early 1920s and 1930s, the Pan-African movement was very strong in Trinidad. Pan-Africanism is the belief that all Africans inside and outside of Africa should unite. Two men from Trinidad, Henry Sylvester Williams and George Padmore, were important figures in this movement. In 1900, Williams set up the first Pan-African Conference in England.

Marcus Garvey, a powerful black leader from nearby Jamaica, was also a Pan-Africanist. Garvey had founded the Universal Negro Improvement Association. This was a worldwide organization with more than 30 chapters in Trinidad. The Pan-African movement in Trinidad formed Stokely's early ideas of politics.

Back-to-Africa movement leader Marcus Garvey taught black pride and independence.

When Stokely's Aunt Elaine was asked to remember what Stokely was like as a child, she told the story of something that happened when Stokely was seven. That year, 1948, Trinidad had what was known as a franchise vote for the first time. In order to vote, a person had to be at least 21 years old and own property. One morning Stokely put on his Sunday clothes and slipped out of the house. Albert Gumbs, a neighbor of the Carmichaels', and Uriah Butler were running for office. When Stokely arrived at the polls, he told the people in charge that he wanted to vote. They asked him how old he was. Stokely replied that he was seven. "Oh, too young," he was told. "You need to be 21."

Stokely was disappointed, but he went home determined to get his Aunt Elaine to vote. Aunt Elaine hadn't planned to vote. Stokely kept telling her, "You must vote! You must vote!" He even told her to vote for Butler. Butler was Stokely's favorite candidate because he had gone to jail for the people. Uriah Butler was a tremendous force among the black people in Trinidad. He called for strikes and was one of the first people to fight the British colonists. In the end, to please Stokely, Aunt Elaine had to vote. This keen interest in politics would always be a part of Stokely's personality.

When he turned 10 in 1951, Stokely entered Tranquility Boys School. He wasn't very happy there because he had left many friends behind at his old school. The British education he received at Tranquility was strict and rigid. The school was also segregated and taught few good things about black people. *Segregated* meant that the black and white children of the island went to separate schools. Stokely was a good student. He was proud of what he learned and often refused help from his Aunt Elaine, who was a teacher.

Toward the end of December 1951, when he was 11, Stokely became very sick with pneumonia. As New Year's Day drew closer, he took a turn for the worse. He had a fever of 103 degrees, and his breathing was no more than a thin, raspy sound. A doctor was called. Young Stokely was so sick that the doctor didn't expect him to live through the night. By daybreak, however, he was out of danger. Fourteen days later, while Stokely was still recovering, his grandmother, Lynette Emelda, died. Young Stokely took this very hard. Little did he know that 1952 would bring many more changes into his life. The balmy, easygoing days of his childhood in Trinidad were about to come to an end.

On June 14, 1952, Stokely and his three sisters left Trinidad and joined their parents in the United States. Thirty years would pass before he returned to the place of his birth. In the meantime, Stokely said good-bye to the members of his family who stayed behind in the safe world of Trinidad that he knew so well. Stokely had a spirit of adventure, though. He looked forward to joining his parents and to starting a new life in the United States.

STOKELY COMES OF AGE

> *" Let a new earth rise. Let another world be born.... Let a second generation full of courage issue forth. "*
>
> **MARGARET WALKER ALEXANDER, writer**

The Carmichael family had settled in Harlem, a section of New York City where most of the people are black. Many words have been used in the United States to describe blacks, or African Americans. Depending upon how a word was used, it could be insulting or reflect pride. These words include *colored*, *Negro*, *people of color*, *black*, and *African American*. What a different world Harlem was for Stokely. In this new world, blacks did not own their own land. Store owners and landlords were white. Stokely was curious about and excited by the differences between his old home and the new one. He was excited by the fast life in Harlem. He quickly fit right in and began to make new friends.

During much of the 20th century, Harlem has been a beacon drawing black people from all over the world. This part of the United States has had great political, artistic, and cultural importance for blacks. Later, Stokely said that Harlem "represented life, real life. On one block you have a church and right next door is a bar and they're both packed. On Saturday night people are always in constant motion. You get all of life's contradictions right there in one community: all the wild violence and all the love can be found in Harlem. You get the smells of human sweat and all sorts of bright colors and bright clothes and people in motion. You get preachers on one side of a street and nationalists on the other."

In contrast to the comfortable life he had in Trinidad, Stokely's father now had to struggle to make ends meet. There were now seven people in the family. At night Adolphus Carmichael worked as a cab driver and then went to school to study

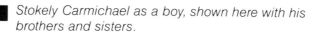

Stokely Carmichael as a boy, shown here with his brothers and sisters.

electricity. During the day, he worked as a carpenter. In an interview for this book, Stokely described his father as a man with "a hardworking nature, [who] never quit before any problem was solved." Elsewhere he said, "...he was head deacon of the church and was so very honest, so very, very honest. He never realized people lied or cheated or were bad. He couldn't conceive of it."

Adolphus Carmichael had an interest in the teachings of Marcus Garvey, the founder of the Universal Negro Improvement Association. He wished he could become involved in politics. But this was impossible for him because he hadn't come into the United States legally. This made it hard for him to join the labor unions that would help him earn better wages.

Stokely's mother, Mabel Carmichael, worked as a maid. Stokely said she "knew...that if you want to make it, you got to hustle and she hustled from the word go. She used to tell me, 'You take nothing from no one, no matter who they are.' She knows the realities of life and she demanded, made sure, that I knew them, too."

After several years, the Carmichael family moved to the Morris Park area of the Bronx in New York City. Stokely recalled: "We came here thinking that this was the promised land. I was eleven years old. We went up to the Bronx and I saw this big apartment house we were going to and I said, 'Wow, Daddy, you own that whole thing?' And then eight of us climbed up to a three-room apartment." This was so different from the way life had been in the fine house Stokely's father had built in Trinidad.

The neighborhood in which the Carmichaels now lived was for the most part made up of white people. For this reason, many of Stokely's friends at this point in his life were white. In fact, Stokely was the only black member of a street gang called the Morris Park Avenue Dukes.

Even though he got into a lot of mischief with the Dukes, Stokely knew that he wanted to go to the Bronx High School of Science. In 1954, just two years before Stokely entered high school, the Supreme Court of the United States made an important ruling. This was the decision to outlaw segregated, or separated, public schools for black and white children. The famous case that led to this ruling was called *Brown* v. *Board of Education*.

The *Brown* v. *Board of Education* case did away with an earlier Supreme Court ruling that had made segregation legal. That case was called *Plessy* v. *Ferguson*. It was decided in 1896 and was known as the "separate but equal" case. At that time, the Court ruled that separation of the races was legal as long as both races had equal public facilities, such as parks and schools. However, far more than public facilities were separate, or segregated. The institutions run by the state or federal government, such as schools and parks, were segregated. Many stores, movie theaters, restaurants, museums, and other businesses were also segregated. The same was true of neighborhoods and city housing.

This system of separating the races was called Jim Crow. Jim Crow was a white entertainer who painted his face black and made fun of African Americans. Jim Crow segregation was at its worst in the South. All over the South were signs marking water fountains and rest rooms White Only and Colored. Blacks could use only those facilities that were marked Colored. They had to use separate entrances to buildings, if they were allowed to enter at all. There were separate black hospitals as well as schools. Blacks even had to step off the sidewalk to let whites pass. They were forced to sit in the back of public buses. And because they were prevented from registering to vote, blacks couldn't change any of these laws.

There were several problems with the "separate but equal" idea. First of all, few of the facilities for blacks were equal in quality to those for whites. The toilets in black rest rooms were often broken or clogged with trash because the city didn't spend money to clean them. Schools were often unheated shacks with no books or learning materials. There were few black hospitals. In an emergency, a black often died before he or she could be taken to the nearest one. Being kept separate also made African Americans feel bad about themselves. They did not feel equal at all.

When *Brown v. Board of Education* outlawed segregation in public schools, people knew that it was only a matter of time before segregation everywhere became illegal, or against the law. This ruling made people who were in favor of segregation very angry.

In August 1955, the anger many whites felt toward blacks made national headlines. Emmett Till, a 14-year-old boy, was visiting his relatives in Money, Mississippi. While he was there, he was brutally murdered by several white men. All he had done was say "Bye, baby" to a white woman in a store. But in the Deep South, blacks weren't supposed to talk to whites that way. The murder drew national attention. Emmett Till's murder reminded people all over the country that a black who dared to talk back to whites or was caught on the white side of town could be in great danger.

Jim Crow laws affected and hurt blacks in many ways. One of the most frustrating results of these laws was that they kept blacks at the lowest economic level in society. Blacks weren't allowed to work at certain high-paying jobs. For example, a black could clean up an office, but he or she could never become a manager there. Many whites wanted to keep things as much as possible just as they were during the days of slavery. They wanted to keep blacks uneducated, feeling bad about themselves, and without the right to vote. In this way, they could keep blacks beneath, or inferior to, them. If blacks existed only to serve them, whites could always think of themselves as the superior race.

But some blacks were beginning to challenge the Jim Crow system. On December 1, 1955, Rosa Parks of Montgomery, Alabama, boarded a bus to go home after work. In those days, blacks had to give up their seats to whites if there weren't enough seats for everyone on the bus. Rosa Parks had worked hard all day, and her feet were tired. That day she refused to give her seat to a white man who was standing. She was arrested for not obeying the law on bus segregation. Parks was already involved in the civil rights work being done by the National Association for the Advancement of Colored People (NAACP). She agreed to allow the NAACP to use her case in the courts to stop segregation.

Four days later, on December 5, 1955, the Montgomery bus boycott began. The black citizens of Montgomery stopped riding the buses. They either walked or organized car pools to get around the city. To help them with their fight, local people found a young minister to be their leader. His name was Martin Luther King, Jr.

More than a year went by before the blacks of Montgomery rode the buses again. This boycott hurt the city's income. During this time, the blacks of Montgomery were constantly threatened by the white community. Martin Luther King, Jr.'s, home was even bombed.

On November 13, 1956, the Supreme Court made segregation on buses illegal. The boycotters in Montgomery had won! This was the most important victory in the growing civil rights movement since *Brown* v. *Board of Education* in 1954. In January 1957, after the Montgomery bus boycott, Martin Luther King, Jr., and 60 other southern black preachers founded the Southern Christian Leadership Conference (SCLC), The SCLC became the organization through which Dr. King waged a nonviolent war against segregation and racism in the United States.

Stokely was still a boy when these events took place. But it would not be long before he, too, became one of the fighters in this movement. At this time, however, he was far from the racial struggle that was going on in the South. For the time being, his biggest challenge was fighting on the streets of New York with the Morris Park Avenue Dukes—and preparing to enter the Bronx High School of Science.

The Bronx High School of Science is one of the best high schools in New York City. In fact, people all over the world know of it. Some of the students there are the children of such professionals as teachers, lawyers, and doctors. In order to get

Highlights in the Life of Stokely Carmichael

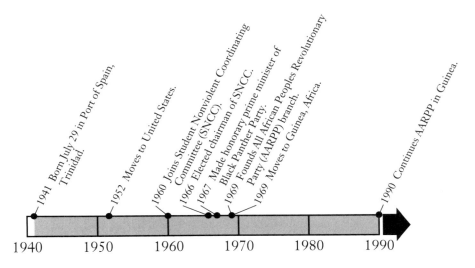

1941 Born July 29 in Port of Spain, Trinidad.

1952 Moves to United States.

1960 Joins Student Nonviolent Coordinating Committee (SNCC).

1966 Elected chairman of SNCC.

1967 Made honorary prime minister of Black Panther Party.

1969 Founds All African Peoples Revolutionary Party (AARPP) branch.

1969 Moves to Guinea, Africa.

1990 Continues AARPP in Guinea.

| 1940 | 1950 | 1960 | 1970 | 1980 | 1990 |

into Bronx Science, students have to take a test that is given in the eighth grade. The Carmichael family didn't find this out until Stokely had already completed the eighth grade. Both the family and Stokely felt so strongly about his going to Bronx Science that he repeated the eighth grade so that he could take the entrance test.

The test was extremely difficult, and very few students who took it passed. Stokely passed the test with flying colors and was admitted to Bronx Science in the fall of 1956. This was a big accomplishment even for someone as bright as Stokely.

Of the 300 students in Stokely's freshman class at Bronx Science, only two were black. Still, there were students from all walks of life. Some, like Stokely, came from working-class families; others were wealthy. This was the first time Stokely got to know middle-class and upper-middle-class whites. At first he was a little scared, but later he made friends with some of his classmates. He also became friends with some young Communist and Socialist students there. In general, Communists and Socialists believe that the government should own everything, but make sure that people have what they need.

While Stokely attended an integrated high school in New York City, students in the South were still battling against segregated schools. Little Rock, Arkansas, became the center of national attention when nine black students tried to integrate Central High School there. Following the Supreme Court ruling on *Brown* v. *Board of Education*, a federal court ordered Little Rock to integrate its schools. The Little Rock Nine, as the black students were called, were to enter Central High School in September 1957. The governor of Arkansas, Orval Faubus, declared "Blood will run in the streets" if black children tried to integrate the school.

On September 3, the first day of school, Faubus placed 250 National Guardsmen outside the school to deal with possible riots. For protection, Daisy Bates, the president of the state's NAACP, arranged to take the nine children to school together. But she was unable to reach one child, 15-year-old Elizabeth Eckford.

When Elizabeth approached the school she was met with a jeering mob of angry whites. She walked toward the line of guards to enter the school, but they wouldn't let her through. Then the mob began shouting, "Lynch her! Lynch her!" Everywhere she turned the mob followed her, screaming curses and threats and spitting on her. At last a friendly white woman helped her get on a nearby bus, and she got away. The other eight students hadn't been able to get through the line of National Guardsmen either. That day, Central High School wasn't integrated.

For more than two weeks, the Little Rock Nine weren't able to enter Central High School. Each time they tried, the whites threatened to riot. Governor Faubus refused to remove the National Guardsmen. On September 23, the students managed to get in through a side entrance. Someone in the crowd shouted, "Oh, my God, they're in the school!" and began weeping. Since the black students were out of their reach, the mob began beating white journalists who were reporting on the integration. The mob grew to about 1,000 people before the black students were removed for their own safety.

One of the students, Melba Pattillo, remembers that day.

They were put into the backseat of a car in the basement of the school. Just before he drove out into the crowd, the policeman who was driving the students home told them to keep their heads down. Out of the window, Melba "could just see hands reaching across this car. I could hear the yelling. I could see guns. The driver didn't hit anybody, but he certainly was force-ful...in the way he exited this driveway because people tried to stop him. He dropped me off at home, and I remember saying, 'Thank you for the ride.' I should have said, 'Thank you for my life.'"

Finally, President Dwight D. Eisenhower sent more than 1,000 federal troops to Little Rock. The National Guardsmen were ordered to defend the black students instead of frightening them. The Little Rock Nine were escorted to school by jeeps mounted with machine guns. It was plain to see that even though the Supreme Court had ruled that segregation was ille-gal, integration wouldn't happen overnight. Black Americans would need better legislation, or laws, to ensure that they had the same rights enjoyed by white Americans.

That same month Congress passed the 1957 Civil Rights Act. This act created the Civil Rights Commission to advise the president on issues concerning African Americans. It also gave the government the right to sue registration offices if they dis-criminated against blacks over voting rights. But the Civil Rights Act didn't give the government the power to enforce school desegregation laws or other laws that had already been passed to protect the rights of African Americans. Most African Americans weren't happy with this act. It was the first civil rights legislation since the Civil War ended. But it didn't go far enough toward giving African Americans their rights or pro-tecting them from racist whites who felt they shouldn't have these rights.

Soon Stokely would become a part of this new civil rights movement to give blacks the power they needed. Meanwhile, he was learning many new things at Bronx Science. Stokely loved the competition there and was always looking for new chal-

lenges. He found that the extra year he spent in the eighth grade hadn't been wasted. He dived into his studies and did well. He liked to listen to Bach and other composers of classical music. He was also exposed to such modern writers and thinkers as Albert Camus, Jean-Paul Sartre, and Karl Marx during this time. He began to explore the world of politics, too. Stokely attended meetings of the Young Communists, the youth group of the Communist party.

In late 1959, relations between the United States and Cuba weren't good. The United States stopped buying sugar from Cuba because Cuba took U.S. property there. This was a boycott, and it had a bad effect on the national income of Cuba. To protest this boycott, Stokely took part in a group called Fair Play for Cuba.

The United States wasn't the promised land Stokely thought it would be. Still, he took advantage of the best his new home had to offer.

3 THE CALL

❝ I am a descendant, an heir to a legacy of struggle. I am movement evoked, movement evolved. ❞

EUGENE REDMOND, poet

With only five months to go before graduation, Stokely was trying to decide which college to attend. But two events occurred in 1960 that would influence and change the course of his life forever. These events touched Stokely so deeply that he had to get involved. He became a political activist. First, there were the student sit-ins. These sit-ins made Stokely more aware of what it meant to be black. The second event was the creation of the Student Nonviolent Coordinating Committee (SNCC, pronounced *snick*). SNCC was made up of students who organized the sit-ins.

A sit-in is a form of protest. People who took part in the civil rights movement protested against bad treatment by sitting at segregated lunch counters or on the floor of public places. These acts of protest were called civil disobedience. The sit-ins came about because southern black students were impatient with the SCLC and the NAACP. The students felt that these organizations weren't achieving equality fast enough. African-American students also felt a growing sense of black pride as they watched countries in Africa achieve independence. During 1960, more than 11 African countries won their freedom from European colonial rule. African Americans began to ask what they could do to change their place in American society. Blacks in the South lived in much the same way blacks in South Africa lived under apartheid. *Apartheid* is another word for segregation as it is practiced in South Africa.

On February 1, 1960, Joseph McNeil, Ezell Blair, Jr., Franklin McCain, and David Richmond, four students from North Carolina Agricultural and Technical College, walked into the F. W. Woolworth store in Greensboro, North Carolina. They sat down at the lunch counter. Blacks could stand at the counter, but they weren't allowed to sit down. The whites who worked at the lunch counter asked them to leave and refused to serve them. For these students, just sitting at the counter was a small victory in the battle to get rid of Jim Crow segregation.

The actions of those young black men, all of whom were under age 20, was a planned event that the four students had discussed at college. They had no idea that their sit-in would become a call to other African-American students telling them that they really could do something to change the way they lived.

The call was heard. By the end of that week, hundreds of students—including some whites—had come to sit-in. At that point, the F. W. Woolworth Company closed its doors because service couldn't go on and there was a bomb threat. Within a month, students had staged sit-ins all over the South.

In Nashville, Tennessee, the Nashville Student Movement (NSM) was just beginning its sit-in protests of the lunch counters in that city. The group had been formed by several students who went on to do more work in the civil rights movement. James Lawson, Diane Nash, John Lewis, and James Bevel were among them.

Members of the NSM had trained for nonviolent protest in workshops by role playing. "We would do things like pretend we were sitting at lunch counters, in order to prepare ourselves to do that," recalled Diane Nash. "We would practice things such as how to protect your head from a beating, how to protect each other. If one person was taking a severe beating, we would practice other people putting their bodies in between that person and the violence, so that the violence could be more distributed and hopefully no one would get seriously injured." The NSM was preparing to use these skills they had learned by protesting at department-store lunch counters when they heard about the Greensboro sit-ins.

Most of the students who participated in these sit-ins were polite, peaceful, and very disciplined. It wasn't easy to sit quietly at these lunch counters. Angry whites screamed at the students, threatening them. Often crowds gathered behind the students and spit on them, poured hot coffee over their heads, and ground out cigarettes on their backs. High-school students also took part in the sit-ins. But they were less disciplined and sometimes reacted violently to the abuse they received.

The most important thing about the sit-ins is that they were a direct action against segregation. *Direct action* meant that activists used a nonviolent act such as a sit-in or a march to get results. Previous battles against Jim Crow had been fought by lawsuits in the courtroom. It was true that laws against segregation had been passed. But in the South many blacks still lived under terrible conditions because local governments would not enforce these laws. Direct action forced law officers to finally deal with the new laws.

Those four students from North Carolina Agricultural and Technical College had no idea that their action would inspire so many other students to become involved in the civil rights movement. All through the South—and soon the North—students organized local sit-ins and marches. They formed their own student groups. Many of the students were expelled from college for this protest activity. Some of them were arrested. Worse things happened, too. Students often found themselves in the middle of mobs of angry whites who threatened to kill them.

At first Stokely thought the sit-ins were a publicity trick. Then on TV he saw the students sitting quietly as whites yelled and spit at them and poured ketchup over their heads. It was then that Stokely realized how brave these students were and how much they believed in what they were doing. As he watched them refusing to give in to insults and abuse, a spark lit up in him that would burn for years to come.

A short time afterward, Stokely took part in his first sit-in with the New York chapter of the Congress of Racial Equality (CORE). This sit-in took place in Virginia. He was beaten up during the sit-in, but this abuse just made him want to fight even more.

Finally, after many sit-ins, some of the public places in a number of states were integrated. This meant that blacks could now sit in public eating places that had once been reserved only for whites. But blacks still weren't allowed inside other public places, such as museums, concert halls, or most business offices.

These sit-ins were the first successful mass, or group, action taken by blacks in the South since the Montgomery bus boycott of 1955. One reason they were successful was that many students in many different places participated in them. Another reason the students were able to force change was that the media made the sit-ins national news. Television and newspaper reporters showed pictures of the students patiently sitting day after day. They showed pictures of whites pouring sugar on the protesters. Many people across the country felt the same way Stokely did when he saw pictures of these scenes. Many people were shocked at the behavior of the white racists and proud of the student protesters. The Montgomery bus boycott had also been helped by the press in the same way.

At that time, Ella Baker was the executive director of the SCLC. She wanted to bring these students together and strengthen their leadership skills. She set up the Southwide Youth Leadership Conference at Shaw University in North Carolina on April 15-17, 1960. Shaw University was one of the oldest all-black universities in the United States. It supported many of the students and leaders who took part in the civil rights movement. Martin Luther King, Jr., was the president of the SCLC, but it was Ella Baker who was most involved with the students. Until now, the SCLC and other civil rights organi-

Whites pour sugar, ketchup, and mustard over these sit-in demonstrators in Jackson, Mississippi.

zations had not played a big role in the sit-ins. Ella Baker got $800 from the SCLC to organize the three-day conference at Shaw University. She invited the SCLC, the NAACP, and CORE to take part in the conference. It was here that SNCC (Student Nonviolent Coordinating Committee) was born. The students decided that their organization would be based on the belief of nonviolence. Integration was their goal.

Stokely Carmichael wasn't among the 140 students from 150 southern colleges who attended the conference. At the time, he was participating in CORE pickets against Woolworth's in New York because the company's stores were segregated in the South. In his interview for this book, he recalled: "I followed [the SNCC Conference] through activists in New York. . . . I went to Washington, D.C. . . . to picket. The Washington, D.C., [group] had a sizable [number] of Africans participating. . . . They told me of demonstrations and arrests around desegregation activities in Maryland and Virginia. [Later] I tried to help SNCC in New York."

Both the SCLC and the NAACP wanted the students to join

their groups. But Ella Baker felt that it was important for the students to be independent of the older civil rights groups. She also urged the students to form a "group-centered leadership" instead of a "leader-centered group." The students set up SNCC in a democratic way, with no single person acting as leader of the group. They would all have a say in what the group did. Ella Baker was called the spiritual mother behind the student movement. The Temporary Student Nonviolent Coordinating Committee of SNCC was also formed at the Shaw University conference. The students selected delegates from different colleges to be the central committee for SNCC. Under this plan, the SCLC and CORE agreed to give advice to SNCC.

A few weeks after the conference, on May 1, 1960, a weak Civil Rights Act was signed. It also did little to improve voting rights for African Americans. At that time in the South, only one in four eligible blacks had the power to vote.

On May 13 and 14, 1960, students from across the South came to Atlanta, Georgia, for the first official meeting of SNCC. The SCLC had its main headquarters in Atlanta. Ella Baker knew the students had no funds or office. For this reason, she offered SNCC an office in the SCLC's headquarters. Baker also got Jane Stembridge to run the office. She was a white woman who was studying to be a minister. Later Stembridge and others published the *Student Voice*, SNCC's first newspaper. It was written and designed by the students. The paper printed up-to-date information on student activists and the civil rights movement. It was read in universities throughout the South and the North.

That year, the SNCC delegates—including Marion Barry, who was elected mayor of Washington, D.C., in 1969—were allowed to speak with the platform committees at both the 1960 Democratic and Republican conventions. A platform committee decides what issues the party will support during the election. The SNCC delegates were hardly noticed at the convention. But the fact that they were allowed to voice their opinion there meant a lot. It showed that SNCC was being taken seriously by politicians. SNCC was becoming important, as were other civil rights groups.

Even while he was in high school, Stokely kept up with what was going on in the civil rights movement. In June 1960, he graduated from the Bronx High School of Science. He was offered scholarships to several universities, including Harvard, but he turned them down. Instead he chose to go to Howard University, an all-black school in Washington, D.C. His parents paid for him to go there.

Howard University was thought to be the best university for blacks in the United States. In the eyes of African Americans, Howard ranked as high as Vassar or Harvard did in the eyes of whites. Stokely was eager to study at a black university because of his desire to stay in touch with the movement. He picked premed as his major field of study because he wanted to become a doctor.

Stokely attended Howard in the fall of 1960. There he soon became friends with Bill Mahoney, Courtland Cox, and several others who formed the Nonviolent Action Group (NAG). This group was similar to SNCC. It played an important role in planning demonstrations and sit-ins in Baltimore, Maryland, and Washington, D.C. Stokely still worked with CORE, which also worked closely with NAG. In spite of all his protest activities, Stokely did well in his classes. He was also deeply interested in the national independence movements that were taking place in Africa. Little did Stokely know that within nine years he, too, would be in Africa.

In Atlanta, Georgia, on October 14, 1960, SNCC held its second conference. The gathering was called a leadership conference because one of the organization's goals was to develop leadership skills in young people. The people who attended the conference included the members of 46 protest centers, 140 SNCC delegates from various colleges, and more than 80 observers from other organizations and northern colleges.

The members of SNCC were becoming interested in other issues besides the sit-ins. They wanted to help fight job discrimination. They also decided to stage demonstrations around the upcoming election for president of the United States. They hoped to bring pressure on the candidates and force them to pay attention to the problems of African Americans. The candidates were John F. Kennedy and Richard M. Nixon. SNCC wanted Kennedy and Nixon to take a stand on civil rights issues.

Shortly after the second conference of SNCC, the students persuaded Dr. Martin Luther King, Jr., to join them in a sit-in. Dr. King was arrested and treated badly while he was in jail. When Kennedy learned about this, he made a phone call to the judge who had put King into jail. The day after Kennedy's call, Dr. King was released from jail. This action caused most blacks to give their support to Kennedy in the election. At the end of 1960, the people of the United States voted in John F. Kennedy as their president. Experts say that large numbers of blacks voted for him and helped him to win the election. African Americans hoped that President Kennedy would now pay more attention to their needs.

Even though Stokely was very involved with SNCC and other organizations that used peaceful protests, he didn't agree totally with the idea of nonviolence. He was outraged at the conditions under which blacks lived, especially in the South. Many African Americans felt this anger. Many of them tried to put that anger aside and give their time and energies to such organizations as SNCC. During 1960, SNCC grew in numbers and importance. By the end of the year, 70,000 black students had taken part in sit-ins and marches, and 3,600 had been arrested. There was no turning back now. People across the United States watched as SNCC became more and more involved in the ever-widening struggle for the civil rights of African Americans.

RIDING FOR FREEDOM

*** If you miss me on the back of***
*** the bus,***
*** and you can't find me nowhere,***
*** Come on up to the front of the bus,***
*** I'll be ridin' up there. ***

A song, "If You Miss Me From the
Back of the Bus"

In May 1961, Stokely's first year as a premedical student at Howard University was ending. He had managed to do well in his schoolwork while also being active in NAG. All the pickets and sit-ins Stokely had taken part in that year were good preparation for what he would do later that summer. Few students were prepared for what the summer of 1961 would bring.

Blacks were well aware of the large role the black vote had played in electing John F. Kennedy as president. As a result, blacks expected to see Kennedy pass laws to protect their rights.

One problem blacks in the South wanted changed was segregated interstate, or state-to-state, bus travel. Although local city bus lines were now integrated, blacks still had to ride at the back of the bus when they traveled from one state to another. Often blacks drove together in cars rather than face the embarrassment of having to ride at the back of a bus. Interstate bus travel was controlled by the federal government, so the federal government could do something about integrating it.

In December 1960, the Supreme Court ordered integration of bus stations that served interstate travelers. However, in order for this ruling to mean anything, the Interstate Commerce Commission (ICC) had to agree to enforce it. Now Kennedy had to become involved.

In May 1961, most students were planning to go home or look for summer jobs. Several of them, however, decided to do something entirely different. They joined the Freedom Riders. On May 4, 1961, 13 Freedom Riders left Washington, D.C., on the first Freedom Ride in more than 14 years. The very first rides took place in 1947 and were started by James Farmer of CORE.

The 1961 Freedom Rides were also started by CORE, with Farmer leading the way. The plan was to ride through the Deep South with blacks sitting at the front of the buses and whites sitting at the back. Once they were in a town, the black riders would use the Whites Only rest rooms, and white riders would use those marked Colored. This was to be repeated as the Freedom Riders traveled through Virginia, North Carolina, South Carolina, Louisiana, Alabama, and Mississippi. They planned to arrive in New Orleans, Louisiana, by May 17, the anniversary of the *Brown* v. *Board of Education* decision.

At first the Freedom Riders had no problems as they traveled to different states. But in Atlanta, they divided into two groups to go to Birmingham. When one bus reached Anniston, Alabama, the riders were met by a mob of 30 or 40 angry white people. The Freedom Riders were beaten with lead pipes, baseball bats, iron bats, chains, sticks, clubs, blackjacks, and what-

ever the mob could find. The local police had been standing by. They were just watching what was going on. Finally, they broke up the mob and allowed the bus to go on. The bus got away and stopped six miles outside the town to fix tires that had been slashed. The Freedom Riders were again surrounded by a mob. The mob caught up with them, and someone tossed a firebomb into the back of the bus. The Freedom Riders barely got out of the bus in time.

The bus carrying the other group of Freedom Riders arrived in Birmingham only to be met by another mob. One man was beaten so badly that he lost the use of his legs for the rest of his life. People across the nation were horrified when they read about these attacks in the press. At this point, the bus companies refused to carry the Freedom Riders any farther. They were stranded and had to leave Birmingham by plane. For a time it looked as if violence had triumphed over nonviolence, that the Freedom Riders had been frightened to a standstill.

Before long, though, eight blacks and two whites were on their way to Birmingham to continue the Freedom Rides. As soon as the new Freedom Riders arrived, they were arrested on the spot. The next night around midnight, they were taken from jail by the police officers and dropped at the Alabama-Tennessee border. Eugene "Bull" Connor, Birmingham's public safety commissioner, had ordered this move. Bull Connor was in charge of the police force in Birmingham. Blacks were afraid of Connor. He was known for being brutal toward them. But this didn't stop the brave riders from returning to Birmingham.

For more than a week, the riders couldn't get a bus to take them farther south to Montgomery. Meanwhile, the number of Freedom Riders had risen to 21, as other people came to join them. Most of these people were SNCC workers. The state highway patrol said they would have patrol cars along the highway and a private plane to fly over the bus. The Freedom Riders were ready. They headed for Montgomery.

Stokely was deeply affected by the bravery of the Freedom Riders. After more than a year of being in sit-ins, he wanted to do more for the civil rights movement. He called his mother and told her that he was going to Jackson, Mississippi. Mabel Carmichael wasn't thrilled by the news. She gave in, however, when Stokely reminded her that he was putting his life on the line to end segregation. Two weeks later, Stokely was among the Freedom Riders who entered Mississippi with the help of CORE. He later recalled: "I came in with the group from New Orleans on the train into Jackson, Mississippi, two weeks after the first bus went through Anniston. CORE wanted to call off the Freedom Rides but we in SNCC insisted."

On May 24, 1961, the Freedom Riders left Montgomery, Alabama, to go to Jackson, Mississippi. When Stokely and the other Freedom Riders tried to enter a white cafeteria and rest rooms, they were arrested for violating state laws. The Freedom Riders were put on trial and found guilty of disturbing the peace. They were sentenced to 60 days in the state prison. When Stokely decided to take part in the Freedom Rides, he was probably prepared to experience some type of violence. But this was his first arrest and his first time in jail.

Stokely and the other Freedom Riders stayed in the Parchman Penitentiary in Mississippi for 53 days. During this time, they lived under terrible conditions: dirty mattresses, food that was so bad they couldn't eat it, and constant torment from prison guards. Often the men were put in handcuffs called wristbreakers. They were poked with electric rods called cattle prods. This was very, very painful. At one point, the sheriff had 10 fans and an air conditioner placed in front of the jail cells. He also removed the mattresses from the cells. Most of the Freedom Riders weren't wearing much clothing. With 10 fans and an air conditioner blowing, the temperature often went down to 30 degrees. They were freezing. This was done for days at a time.

Stokely recalled being at Parchman:

> I'll never forget this Sheriff Tyson—he used to wear those big boots. He'd say, " ... I'm going to see to it that you

don't ever get out of this place." They decided to take our mattresses because we were singing...And then they put wristbreakers on Freddy Leonard...and Tyson said, "Oh, you want to hit me, don't you," and Freddy just looked up at him meekly and said, "No, I just want you to break my arm." ... I hung on to my mattress and said, "I think we have a right to them and I think you're unjust," ... and [he] started to put on the wristbreakers. I wouldn't move and I started to sing "I'm Gonna Tell God How You Treat Me," and everybody started to sing it and by this time Tyson was really to pieces.

The prisoners weren't allowed to read or have any exercise. They had nothing to do for days and days. One way that the Freedom Riders helped themselves was by singing. Singing lifted their spirits. The Freedom Riders became known for the brave way in which they sang the freedom songs. Sometimes they made up funny words to songs, such as this one about the prison:

> Mine eyes have seen the disintegration of my underwear.
> Every time I put them on I seem to find another tear
> Pretty soon I'll be walking round with my bottom bare
> It's the Parchman fashion flair.

This kind of singing often brought harsh treatment from the guards, but that didn't stop the Freedom Riders from singing.

The Freedom Riders had different political views and experiences. For this reason, there were disagreements and debates among them. For example, those who weren't religious refused to take part in the prayer sessions that were held in the cells. More than two-thirds of the Freedom Riders were college students. Three-fourths of them were males, and more than half were blacks from the South. Many were ministers and rabbis. In spite of these differences, they worked together as a loyal, unified group of brave protesters.

By the end of the summer, 328 people had been arrested in

Jackson, Mississippi. But they refused to give in. In fact, just the opposite happened. Putting the Freedom Riders in jail made more protesters want to take a Freedom Ride to Mississippi. They filled the jails and refused to pay bail money to get out.

On September 22, 1961, President Kennedy finally ordered the ICC to issue a ruling. According to this ruling, separate facilities for blacks and whites—rest rooms, waiting rooms, and so on—were against the law. This law was supposed to become effective on November 1, 1961, but several southern communities ignored the ruling. Workers from SNCC and Freedom Riders continued to test the law. In Shreveport, Louisiana, Jackson, Mississippi, and Albany, Georgia, no one seemed to be obeying the law. In McComb, Mississippi, SNCC workers were attacked by a violent mob.

The Ku Klux Klan was (and still is) a group of violent whites who believed that they were better than blacks and that the two races should remain separate. They believed in using violence to keep blacks "in their places." They were known for beating and killing blacks and for burning crosses on their lawns. They joined the mobs who attacked black protesters. The mobs burned buses and beat students so badly that some of them had to be sent to the hospital. Many students ended up in jail or were run out of the towns where they were attending school.

After spending 53 days in Parchman Penitentiary, Stokely barely got back to Howard University in time for the fall term. His mother recalled that he barely had time to go home and have his hair cut before he was on his way back to school. But for Stokely, there was no turning back. In Mississippi, he had been right in the middle of the civil rights movement. From now on, he knew that the movement would be his life.

AT THE CROSSROADS, MARCHING FOR FREEDOM

"Hey, Mr. Kennedy, take us out of misery,
Freedom's coming and it won't be long,
This evil segregation, look what it has done to me.
Freedom's coming and it won't be long."

A song written by members of CORE

During his second year at Howard University, Stokely decided that "medicine was not my calling." He changed his major to philosophy, which is the study of how people think and believe. He phoned his mother and told her that he "would rather heal people before they get sick."

Adolphus Carmichael was somewhat disappointed because he wanted his son to be a doctor. However, Stokely had different plans. He said, "Philosophy excited me—it taught me to think and struggle with ideas."

During the early part of 1962, Adolphus Carmichael died at the age of 42. For him, the American dream never came true. Stokely felt bitter about his father's death. He believed that America had just "squashed" his father. Now Stokely was the man of the family. He took his father's death very hard and had to be coaxed to go home for the funeral. He had always admired his father's "sterling honesty [and] hard-working nature." However, he didn't want to live in the world the way his father had lived. Mabel Carmichael remembered: "Stokely went to Howard University under my circumstances. Stokely did not want help from the NAACP." There were two Carmichael children in college at this time. One of them would have to drop out because of the financial burden caused by their father's death. Stokely's sister decided to finish her education at a later time, while he remained at Howard University. From time to time, he received a small scholarship from the National Association of Negro Women to help him with his expenses.

Across the South, blacks were chipping away at the rock of segregation. Conditions for blacks in the United States were difficult, almost hopeless. Twice as many blacks as whites were out of work, and blacks earned about half as much money as whites did.

In Albany, Georgia, conditions seemed even worse. The black population was extremely poor, and the town was run by a white majority. SNCC went to Albany in the summer of 1961. The students wanted to help organize the black community there. One of the few rights Albany blacks had was the ICC ruling. This ruling made segregation of interstate and public train and bus stations illegal. SNCC workers decided to test the law. As soon as they entered the Whites Only sections, the police forced them out of the station.

On November 22, 1961, SNCC and the NAACP staged a demonstration at the bus station in Albany. Five people were arrested. The NAACP workers were released, but two of the SNCC activists decided not to pay bail and remained in jail. The arrests brought Albany blacks together. They held their first mass rally on November 25, 1961. On December 10, protesters tried to integrate the bus station. Their arrests sparked a mass march by students in SNCC. In all, 267 students were arrested for refusing to end their march. Many of them were expelled by their schools for having been arrested.

Dr. William Anderson was the president of a group of local organizations known as the Albany Movement. He asked Martin Luther King, Jr., to help them. King went to Albany and spoke at a big meeting held at the Shiloh Baptist Church. He had planned to leave the next day, but the leaders of the Albany Movement asked him to stay and lead a march. King was so moved by the people of Albany that he agreed. He was arrested during that march, along with 250 other protesters. He decided to stay in Albany's jail until the city was desegregated. SNCC activists were angry about King's decision to stay. They felt that he was trying to take over the movement that they had been building for many weeks.

At first the blacks in Albany only wanted to desegregate the bus station, but they now began to ask themselves, Why not desegregate the whole town? Why not integrate lunch counters, the city parks, and schools, too?

To get rid of the protesters, the mayor of Albany, Asa Kelley, and other city officials made a deal with local black leaders. The city agreed to integrate the bus and train stations. They also told blacks that they could have a meeting with the Albany city council. They also said they would release all the marchers from jail if the demonstrators called off their protests. When the local blacks agreed to the deal, the city released all the protesters.

As soon as King and his marchers were out of jail, however, the city officials refused to integrate the bus and train stations.

They also refused to meet with the demonstrators. In addition, they managed to make King look bad in front of the press. Reporters thought King knew about the deal that had been made between the city and the local black leaders. Now he looked bad in the public's eyes. Since he was no longer in jail, King lost his bargaining position. The media weren't so eager to cover him if he wasn't in jail.

Police Chief Laurie Pritchett was just as wily as the city officials had been. He was afraid that if King stayed in town, things would get worse. The national media had already looked very closely at the movement in Albany. The police chief decided to beat King at his own game. He would be nonviolent, too. That way, the protesters would look bad on the TV news—not him. Then King wouldn't get any sympathy for his cause.

Every time the protesters demonstrated, Chief Pritchett usually arrested them for loitering or disturbing the peace. He wouldn't arrest them for breaking segregation laws and give the media a chance to discuss those laws. He transported protesters to nearby county jails so that the demonstration leaders could never fill the jails in Albany as they had hoped to do. With all the jails filled, the officials would have been unable to make any more arrests. They would have had to give in to the protesters. He treated the marchers nonviolently and even gave King police protection. Chief Pritchett looked good in front of the national TV cameras.

This kind of trickery went on in Albany for almost a year and a half. Finally, in August 1962, King left Albany. He had been unable to beat the white city officials at the game they were playing. Albany's schools remained segregated. The city closed its parks so that it wouldn't have to integrate them. After the library was integrated, all the chairs inside were removed so that no whites would have to sit next to blacks. Many people thought the Albany Movement would die when King left. However, William Anderson, head of the Albany Movement, and many Albany citizens felt it was a great success. Anderson felt that there was a change in the attitude of local blacks, especially those who participated in the movement. Albany would never again be the same. The seeds of change had taken hold there.

There were several reasons why the Albany Movement didn't have immediate success. First, Police Chief Laurie Pritchett and Mayor Asa Kelley frustrated King's plans by outsmarting him. Another important reason was the lack of unity between the black groups that were working in Albany. The members of SNCC resented the way Dr. King and the SCLC just swooped in and took all the attention. Many of the students felt that if the SCLC had simply sent them money and King had come to the city to speak and walk with the marchers, that would have been enough.

The SCLC leaders saw the situation differently, however. They felt that SNCC and the other activists didn't have enough experience to organize a whole city movement. They thought they had to come to SNCC's rescue. One SCLC leader resented SNCC's attitude toward King and the SCLC. He said SNCC wanted the national attention that Dr. King attracted, but they didn't want his organization—the SCLC—to give them one word of advice.

SNCC remained in Albany and continued its work of organizing for six more years. Its members learned many valuable lessons in Albany about how to organize a community. They would be able to use these lessons later in other places.

By the fall of 1962, Stokely was in his third year at Howard University. As a leader in NAG, he took part in demonstrations and pickets in Cambridge, Maryland, near Howard. That fall, Stokely watched as James Meredith became the first black to enter the University of Mississippi. This wasn't easy for Meredith, a former staff sergeant in the U.S. Air Force. He knew the history of Ole Miss, as the university was called.

Ole Miss was one of the best places to get an education in the South, but the university wouldn't dream of opening its doors to black students. Its policy of totally excluding blacks had deprived them of an opportunity to receive the same top-quality education offered to many whites. Meredith wanted to study engineering. He had completed courses at the all-black Jackson State College, but he wanted to finish up at Ole Miss. Meredith asked Medgar Evers, field secretary of the NAACP, for help in entering Ole Miss. Medgar Evers talked to Thurgood Marshall, the head of the NAACP Legal Defense Fund. Marshall took the case to court. Meredith's efforts drew national attention. Finally, on September 3, 1962, President Kennedy ordered the courts to have Ole Miss integrated.

On September 30, 1962, 123 deputy marshals, 316 border patrolmen, and 97 federal prison guards stood in front of the Ole Miss administrative building. Meanwhile, James Meredith was secretly taken to his dormitory. Twenty-four federal agents stood outside his room to guard him. A mob of angry whites began to riot at the administration office. They thought Mer-

James Meredith, seen upon his successful entrance to Ole Miss.

edith would be entering the campus there. By the end of the night, two men lay dead and 375 had been injured in the campus riots. The rioters never once suspected that James Meredith was already on campus. The next day, Meredith signed up as a student at Ole Miss. He said, "In the past the Negro has not been allowed to receive the education he needs. If this is the way it must be [done], and I believe it is, then it is not too high a price to pay."

In 1962, education wasn't the only right that was denied blacks in Birmingham, Alabama. The black community and the white community there seemed to be at war. Most of the public facilities, such as parks, schools, and libraries, were closed. They had been closed to avoid obeying the Supreme Court's order to integrate them. There had been 18 bombings in the black part of town over a six-year period. In addition, blacks made up 40 percent of the population in Birmingham, yet few of them had ever voted. They earned less than half the amount of money earned by whites, and they were three times less likely to have a high-school education or any kind of technical training.

In January 1963, Martin Luther King, Jr., and other members of the SCLC decided to help Rev. Fred Shuttlesworth of Birmingham plan a protest against the segregation in Birmingham. Shuttlesworth was the head of a local group called the Alabama Christian Movement for Human Rights. This plan became known as Project "C" ("C" stood for confrontation). It was launched in March 1963 in Birmingham.

In April, 20 blacks were arrested in Birmingham for picketing a department store. For several days, there were marches and pickets. King and 50 other people marched into downtown Birmingham, where they were arrested. King was placed in solitary confinement, which meant that he had to stay in a small jail cell alone. This was a harsh punishment. While he was in jail, King wrote his famous "Letter from a Birmingham Jail." This letter was his answer to another letter from white clergymen. In it King explained why blacks could no longer wait for their freedom.

Soon after King was released, the movement began to lose power because marchers weren't able to go to jail. Many of them had been in jail for so long that they were being fired from their jobs. James Bevel was an experienced SNCC activist. He suggested that King use children instead of adults in the marches. Adults weren't able to march because they were afraid of losing their jobs. But children didn't have to worry about that. Bevel also felt that children would be more fearless and would wake up the conscience of the people of the United States. Finally, King agreed to do this.

On May 2, the first protest march using children started out from the Sixteenth Street Baptist Church. The children who took part in the march ranged from 6 to 18 years of age. By the end of that day, 959 children had been arrested. The following day, more than 1,000 children left school to march. This time Public Safety Commissioner Eugene "Bull" Connor used police dogs and fire hoses on the children. These fire hoses had enough force to rip the bark from trees. The force of the water slammed the marchers into buildings and parked cars. By Monday, May 6, the jails in Birmingham were filled with 2,000 marchers. Dr. King came under attack from many people who felt that he should not use children to march because it was too dangerous.

The marches in Birmingham drew the attention of people from all over the world. Scenes from Birmingham that appeared on TV shocked Americans and made them feel ashamed that people could be treated so badly in this country. President Kennedy had no power in Birmingham, even though he wanted to send in soldiers. This was a state matter. The children kept marching even though police dogs attacked them and fire hoses knocked them down. Finally, Bull Connor's men, some of them weeping, refused to obey his order to stop the children. Kennedy sent Assistant Attorney General Burke Marshall to Birmingham. Marshall got King and the white leaders of Bir-

PROTEST DEMONSTRATIONS IN THE SOUTH

Bus Boycott

Demonstrations

Freedom Ride Stop

March

Student Sit-ins

School Integration

★ State Capital

Washington, D.C.

Richmond ★
VIRGINIA

Raleigh ★
NORTH CAROLINA

Greensboro

Frankfort ★
KENTUCKY

Knoxville ★

Nashville
TENNESSEE

Columbia ★
SOUTH CAROLINA

ATLANTIC OCEAN

St. Augustine

FLORIDA

Atlanta ★
GEORGIA

Anniston

Birmingham

Albany

Tallahassee ★

Memphis

Tuscaloosa
ALABAMA

Montgomery ★

Selma

Oxford
MISSISSIPPI

Meridian

Mobile

Jackson ★

Little Rock ★
ARKANSAS

LOUISIANA

Baton Rouge ★

New Orleans

GULF OF MEXICO

N
W   E
S

0   100   200
miles

mingham together to reach an agreement. The result of this agreement was that lunch counters, rest rooms, and drinking fountains would be desegregated. Also, blacks would be hired for jobs.

Several weeks after this, President Kennedy presented a new civil rights bill to Congress. Civil rights leaders decided to hold a march on Washington, D.C., to pressure Congress into passing the bill. A. Philip Randolph was called to organize the march. In 1941, Randolph had organized a march to demand more jobs for African Americans in the defense plants that were preparing the United States for World War II. That march was called off when President Franklin Delano Roosevelt declared that there would be no employment discrimination in federal plants. Roosevelt also established the Fair Employment Practices Committee.

Nearly 20 years before that march, in 1925, Randolph had founded the Brotherhood of Sleeping Car Porters. A sleeping car porter worked on the railroad trains, serving passengers. The brotherhood was the first black labor union to be formed in the United States. Since that time, Randolph had been fighting for the rights of African Americans. In fact, other black leaders called him the father of the civil rights movement.

The March on Washington was called to put pressure on Congress to pass a new Civil Rights Act. It was also called to bring attention to the need for integration in the nation's public schools. Just as important were demands for fair employment, an end to job discrimination, and the integration of interstate public facilities. Dr. King, the SCLC, SNCC, the NAACP, and CORE all supported this march. Everyone wanted to see the new bill passed.

As the march was being planned, a terrible thing happened. Medgar Evers, a field secretary for the NAACP, was killed outside his home in Jackson, Mississippi, on June 12. The death of this brave, gentle man was a terrible blow to the black community. African Americans were so angry about his death that the Kennedy administration feared that the March on Washington would turn into a riot. It did not. It ended up as one of the most wonderful chances for blacks and whites to come together. They came together because they believed that all Americans were equal—no matter what the color of their skin.

On the day of the march, August 28, 1963, the organizers hoped that 100,000 people would turn out. Instead, 250,000 came! People of all colors, religious beliefs, and all walks of life showed up. Under bright-blue skies in a big green park in Washington, D.C., Martin Luther King, Jr., made one of the most famous speeches of all time. This was his "I Have a Dream Speech." He said:

> I am not unmindful that some of you have come here out of great trials and tribulations. Some of you have come fresh from narrow jail cells. Some of you have come from areas where your quest for freedom left you battered by the storms of persecution and staggered by the winds of police brutality. . . . I say to you today, my friends, so even though we face the difficulties of today and tomorrow, I still have a dream. It is a dream deeply rooted in the American meaning of its creed, "We hold these truths to be self-evident, that all men are created equal." I have a dream that one day on the red hills of Georgia, sons of former slaves and the sons of former slave owners will be able to sit down together at the table of brotherhood. . . . I have a dream that my four little children will one day live in a nation where they will not be judged by the color of their skin, but the content of their character. . . .

John Lewis, the chairman of SNCC, was also invited to speak at the March on Washington. Some people thought his speech was too full of anger, however. The Roman Catholic archbishop of Washington said he would not be in the march unless Lewis's speech was changed. Lewis agreed to change his speech. This is what he ended up saying:

> We march today for jobs and freedom, but we have nothing to be proud of, for hundreds and thousands of our brothers

are not here—for they have no money for their transportation, for they are receiving starvation wages . . . or no wages at all. . . . For the first time in 100 years this nation is being awakened to the fact that segregation is evil and it must be destroyed in all forms. . . . I want to know—which side is

the federal government on? . . . The revolution is a serious one. Mr. Kennedy is trying to take the revolution out of the streets and put it in the courts. Listen, Mr. Kennedy, listen, Mr. Congressman, listen, fellow citizens—the black masses are on the march for jobs and freedom, and we must say to the politicians that there won't be a "cooling-off period."

Lewis became the militant, or aggressive, spokesman for the youth of the movement. Many young blacks were demanding a more militant stand from the leaders.

While the March on Washington was going on, Stokely was attending a National Student Association conference. "NAG was asked to have someone elected to [the] student body so SNCC could have official voice," he said. "I was chosen to run. It is the only student elected position I ever ran for. As an official representative to NSA and of course being [a member of] SNCC it was absolutely necessary that I go to the conference which was the same date as the march." Stokely shared the feelings of other SNCC activists about the march. "I knew the march would [unite] and [inspire] the people, which it did. I [also] knew nothing concrete would come out of it," he said.

Stokely was right about the march inspiring people. Those who went, as well as many throughout the nation who could only watch from their TV sets, gathered hope from the march. The hope was that change could really happen in this country. He may also have been right about nothing coming from the march. No one knows how the march affected Congress. The Civil Rights Act wasn't passed for nearly a year. And worse, violence erupted only weeks after the march took place.

On September 15, four little girls were killed when a bomb was thrown into the Sixteenth Street Baptist Church in Birmingham. America may have stood still and listened during the March on Washington, but southern whites were still waging a hateful war against blacks in the South.

MISSISSIPPI FREEDOM DEMOCRATIC PARTY

" Over my head, Oh, Lord,
I see freedom in the air,
Over my head I see freedom in the air,
There must be a God somewhere. "

From a song written by members of
the Albany Movement

Stokely Carmichael graduated from Howard University in May 1964. He had been offered a scholarship to go to Harvard University to begin work on advanced degrees. But he turned down the offer without a second thought. For Carmichael, the civil rights movement had become a way of life. It had taken hold of his goals and become the fuel that gave energy to his actions. He had no doubt that his work for the movement would continue. Right now, important civil rights changes were taking place in Mississippi.

On July 2, the 1964 Civil Rights Act was signed into law by President Lyndon B. Johnson, who had become president after the assassination of President Kennedy in November 1963. The passage of this law was an important victory for the civil rights movement. Under this law, segregation in all private and public places was now illegal. It outlawed discrimination in jobs and by labor unions. However, the law did not do enough to secure voting rights for African Americans in the South. For example, in Mississippi only a few blacks of voting age were registered to vote. They had been kept out of the "whites only" Mississippi Democratic party, which had influence all over the state. The Mississippi Democratic party did not allow blacks to register or attend any of its meetings.

African Americans in Mississippi knew they could not work with the racist Mississippi Democratic party. On July 28, 1964, the party adopted this statement as its state plan: "We oppose, condemn and deplore the Civil Rights Act of 1964. . . . We believe in separation of the races in all [parts] of our society. It is our belief that the separation of the races is necessary for the peace and [the good] of all the people of Mississippi. . . . "

SNCC workers had been in Mississippi since the summer of 1961 helping African Americans there gain the right to vote. Things were so bad in this part of the country that the last time African Americans had voted was right after the Civil War. SNCC worked in Mississippi along with the SCLC, CORE, and the NAACP. All of these groups got together to form the Council of Federated Organizations (COFO). SNCC was the driving force behind COFO. In 1963, COFO created the Freedom Vote. The Freedom Vote was a make-believe election in which Freedom Party candidates competed against the Republican and Democratic candidates. In putting on this pretend election, the Freedom Party hoped to show the federal government and the state of Mississippi that African Americans had made up their minds that they were going to vote. The Freedom Vote elections also gave African Americans practice in casting the ballot. In the elections, a total of 80,000 people came out to vote.

The Freedom Party had been very successful, so SNCC decided to prepare Mississippi's African-American population for a real election. The year 1964 was another year in which a president of the United States would be elected. A big effort was made to get young college students from across the United States to help register voters. This huge voter-registration drive took place in the summer of 1964. It was called the Mississippi Freedom Summer Project.

The Mississippi Freedom Summer Project set up centers in towns to give legal and medical assistance to African Americans. Freedom schools, freedom clinics, and other programs made up the Mississippi Freedom Summer Project.

SNCC helped to form the Mississippi Freedom Democratic Party (MFDP) in April 1962. Giving the party this name was a real challenge. The party wanted to be seen as the real Democratic party for the state of Mississippi. The challenge was to beat the Mississippi Democratic party, which was open only to whites. The MFDP's goal was to install a party in Mississippi that was truly democratic.

One of the founders of the MFDP was Fannie Lou Hamer. Hamer refused to give in to the many acts of violence that were directed against her when she tried to register to vote. Once she was beaten so badly that she could not walk. Then she lost her home. Hamer became a national legend at the 1964 Democratic National Convention in Atlantic City, New Jersey. In front of TV cameras, she told her story to people across the United States. Her ability to speak simply and honestly about the conditions under which she and other African Americans lived and about her deep desire to vote won the hearts of the nation. She had given all she had for the right to vote. She later became a SNCC organizer and one of the most important people in the MFDP.

In many ways, Fannie Lou Hamer was the symbol of the MFDP. Carmichael and other SNCC workers were greatly influenced and inspired by Hamer's determination and strength. To Carmichael, "working with Fannie Lou Hamer and others like her was like being constantly inspired." Carmichael was also inspired by the blacks in Mississippi. Their simple bravery

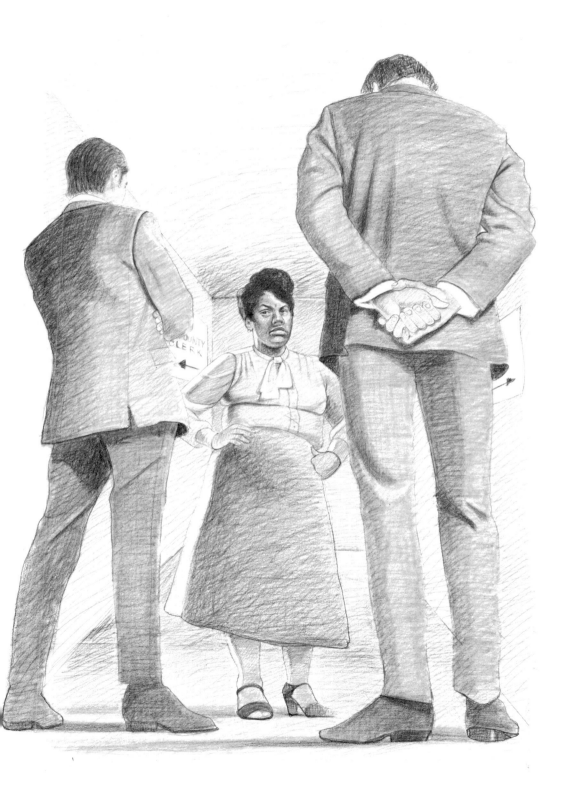

in the face of brutal violence from whites moved him. He felt they were honest and "pure," and that "even sinners must have [respect] for purity."

One of the goals of COFO was to get the Mississippi Freedom Democratic Party ready for the 1964 Democratic National Convention. Bob Moses was the chief SNCC organizer for the Mississippi Freedom Summer Project. Moses was involved in recruiting, or finding, students to work for the program. He felt that there were four main goals of the Freedom Summer Project. The first was to register blacks in Mississippi to vote. The second was to organize a legal Democratic party. A third goal was to establish freedom schools to teach reading and math to black children. Freedom Summer workers also wanted to open community centers where poor blacks could get legal and medical assistance. These and other programs made up the Mississippi Freedom Summer Project.

In the beginning, more than 800 students received training to go to Mississippi. Many of them came from the northeastern part of the country. More than half of them were white, and about 300 of them were women. Their average age was 21. Each volunteer had to bring $500 for bail, plus enough cash to cover his or her living expenses. They also had to take care of their own medical bills and transportation home at the end of the summer. Most of the students came from families that were fairly well-off. During the training, it became clear that black staff members and white COFO student volunteers did not agree about everything. There was tension over the differences between the two races. These differences of opinion could not be erased during a one-week training course.

Carmichael had become more and more aware of the problems of having white workers in the movement. He felt that it would be easier for black workers to educate the local blacks and help them to overcome their fears. White freedom workers had to be sensitive to everyday black life. This wasn't easy because the black community was a closed community that had learned not to trust whites. The local blacks also had serious doubts about the changes the COFO workers spoke of.

At first SNCC felt that a large number of whites coming into Mississippi might weaken the power base of the local blacks. However, the blacks there felt that the help of the students would be a good thing. The students were trained in groups of 200 to 300 people at a time. The first wave of volunteers arrived in Mississippi in May 1964. When Carmichael graduated from

Stokely Carmichael teaches a group of students about resistance skills and political awareness.

Howard University, he, too, joined the Mississippi Freedom Summer Project. He became the head of the SNCC and COFO office for one of the voting districts in Mississippi. As head of this office, his duties involved finding and training staff people, registering people to vote, giving out funds, and holding community meetings. He also stayed in close contact with other district offices.

Everyone who worked for the Mississippi Freedom Summer Project had to face the fact that the job was dangerous. A worker might be beaten or killed while doing his or her work. These volunteers did not have the protection of the government and therefore could be attacked at any time by local whites. Even as the volunteers were being trained, the state of Mississippi hired 200 new state-highway patrol officers and bought new military-style equipment. It began to build a new temporary jail, too. The state also made it illegal to give out papers telling about boycotts or to operate a school without a permit. Both of these activities were necessary to the success of the Mississippi Freedom Summer Project. The new laws were created on purpose to make it difficult for SNCC and COFO to do the work they had come to do.

Among the first COFO volunteers were three young men whose tragic end has remained in the minds of Americans for more than 25 years. They were James Chaney, a black CORE member from Mississippi, Andrew Goodman, a white college student from Queens, New York, and Michael Schwerner, a white CORE worker from Brooklyn, New York. The three men disappeared after having been in Meridian, Mississippi, less than two days. They had gone to Meridian to look into the burning of a black church. On the way back, Deputy Sheriff Cecil Price stopped them in Philadelphia, Mississippi, and took them to jail for speeding. They were released later that night, but they were never heard from after that. A huge search took place as the COFO volunteers continued to arrive in Mississippi in large numbers.

On August 4, 1964, 18 days before the Democratic National Convention, the bodies of Chaney, Goodman, and Schwerner were found. They had been shot and buried in a dam on a farm in Philadelphia, Mississippi. Not until December were 21 white men, including the deputy sheriff of Philadelphia, arrested for the murders. A jury found most of those men not guilty.

As time wore on, the Mississippi Freedom Democratic Party won the support of the Michigan and New York delegations to the Democratic National Convention, as well as the backing of the United Auto Workers and the Americans for Democratic Action. In August 1964, more than 800 delegates attended an

MFDP convention in Jackson, Mississippi. SNCC had dedicated most of its time and money to the MFDP. The delegates who went to the Democratic National Convention were Carmichael and SNCC workers Charles McLaurin, Larry Guyot, Fannie Lou Hamer, E. W. Steptoe, Annie Devine, and Hartman Turnbow.

SNCC veterans Ella Baker, Marion Barry, and Reginald Robinson drummed up northern support for the MFDP. President Lyndon B. Johnson didn't take a public stand for or against the MFDP. But it was later learned that he had told the Federal Bureau of Investigation (FBI) to watch the MFDP and SNCC offices during this period.

As soon as the members of the MFDP arrived in Atlantic City, they began passing out leaflets on the life stories of their delegates. They also sent out a legal report that exposed the Mississippi Democratic party as a fake and as an illegal party. The Credentials Committee that had been set up by the national Democratic party would have the job of deciding whether the MFDP could become the official Democratic party of Mississippi.

When it was time for the MFDP to present its case to the Credentials Committee, Fannie Lou Hamer spoke for the party. "If the Freedom Democratic Party is not seated now, I question," she said, "Is this America? The land of the free and the home of the brave?" So powerful was Hamer's speech that President Johnson got nervous because it might disrupt his plans for the convention. He briefly stopped television coverage of the convention. He did this by giving a presidential press conference about the convention so that reporters and TV cameras would switch to covering the news conference instead of the Credentials Committee. This was President Johnson's attempt to erase any image that the Democratic National Convention was under attack. What the MFDP didn't know was that Johnson had already promised the Mississippi governor, Paul Johnson, that no seats would go to the MFDP at the convention.

The Credentials Committee refused to admit the MFDP as the true representative of the people of Mississippi. The Credentials Committee did offer two seats to MFDP delegates, but these seats would not be official. MFDP delegates asked one another whether they should take the two seats. After all, weren't two better than none? But in the end, the MFDP rejected the entire plan. It wanted to represent the state officially at the convention.

That night, on television screens all over the country, there were scenes of Mississippi blacks sitting in seats in the Mississippi section. They had gotten passes from some friendly delegates. One was kicked out, but the rest linked arms. Their supporters moved in and got in the way of the police. Then orders came for the police to stop throwing people out. Afterward, the MFDP celebrated the successful sit-in at a giant rally outside. Some people thought the members of the MFDP weren't very smart when it came to politics. But Carmichael felt differently:

> The lesson in fact, was clear at Atlantic City. . . . Black people in Mississippi and throughout this country could not rely on their so-called allies. Many labor, liberal and civil rights leaders deserted the MFDP because of closer ties to the national Democratic Party. To seat the MFDP over the "regulars" would have meant a displacement of power, and it became crystal clear that in order to combat power, one needed power. Black people would have to organize and obtain their own power base before they could begin to think of coalition with others.

Carmichael left the MFDP shortly after the convention. He was tired of working with whites. He was searching for a new project and a new challenge.

MARION TO SELMA TO MONTGOMERY

> ***Power concedes nothing without demands—it never did and never will.*** ""

FREDERICK DOUGLASS, abolitionist and writer

> ***...it might look like we were just walking down a road, but that was a well organized thing...Marching was a non-violent war.*** ""

ALBERT TURNER, Alabama state director of the SCLC

After Carmichael left the MFDP, he returned to Atlanta, Georgia, for a meeting of SNCC's Executive Committee. He was now convinced that blacks had to form an all-black political party. He believed this was the only way African Americans would ever achieve political power in the

United States. Carmichael, along with SNCC organizers Bob Mants and Willie Vaugn, decided to try to change the political structure in Alabama. They felt that Alabama was the best state in which to try this. Carmichael believed that "once we conquered [Alabama], all the others would be served notice."

Throughout the state of Alabama, blacks felt that if they could vote they would be able to change things for the better. Some blacks were willing to risk everything in order to obtain voting rights. In the cities of Marion and Selma, Alabama, black civil rights workers had begun movements to win their right to vote. SNCC had been in Selma since early 1963. There they continued to work for voter-registration clinics and led marches to the local courthouse to get people registered. Their slogan was "One Man, One Vote." In December 1964, Dr. King announced that he, too, was going to Selma.

White racists in Alabama were very violent about preventing blacks from registering to vote. The sheriff himself, Jim Clark, was well known for beating and jailing marchers. He would even go to other towns to try to scare blacks who were registering to vote. Around Selma, the children and teenagers kept the movement alive by always being available to march while their parents were at work.

Rev. James Anderson (he was the first minister in Selma to allow groups like SNCC to use his church as a gathering place) recalled:

> [The demonstrations] all came about because of unrest among the people because they were being deprived of their constitutional right to vote. I was a college graduate and they wouldn't even let me register. They would find things like something was not legible.... They would ask questions on the Constitution of the U.S., many of which I seriously doubt they could answer. They [also] had delaying tactics. They were determined that they would not register more than a given number of people for a whole

day. That might be five people. Sometimes we had a thousand people out there and couldn't get but five persons registered. That's what motivated the marching.

At the beginning of February 1965, James Orange from the SCLC went to Marion County, Alabama, to work in the voting rights movement there. Each day the blacks would go down to the courthouse to register to vote. There they would be arrested. Over a two-week period, almost 600 people were arrested. In an effort to stop the blacks, the local sheriff arrested Orange on February 17. In response, the local blacks decided to hold a night march. They would go to jail and sing songs to Orange.

Albert Turner, the director of the SCLC in Alabama, remembered that night:

> The mayor of Marion called Governor Wallace and told him that the blacks planned to have a riot that night and wanted to break Mr. Orange out of jail. Wallace sent the state troopers and they deputized a bunch of people. I guess every white man in town that night who wanted to be was deputized.
>
> Their thing that night was to beat us to see if we would stop. They had planned to kill someone. They had all the roads blocked. [Sheriff] Jim Clark left Selma and came up here that night. He had wanted to kill C.T. Vivian who was speaking at the mass meeting that night. (C.T. was slipped out of Marion in an ambulance inside of a casket to hide him from the racist whites.)
>
> After Sheriff Clark could not find C.T. Vivian, he decided they would get all of the blacks in Marion. They had cut the road off and wouldn't let anybody in or out. They beat women. Women had miscarriages in the street that night. They beat up Valeriani [an ABC newscaster]. They took

his news camera and broke it, bust his head, and shot [out] all the lights in town.

They admit themselves that they had planned to murder a black that night. In fact, it could have easily been more than one black. They left several black people for dead, they really thought they were dead.

We left from Zion United Methodist Church which was about two blocks from the Courthouse. We left the church going to the jail. Even before the whole line of people got out of the church, they stopped us. Told us we were unlawfully assembling. The Sheriff of the county had stopped us and asked me if I was an outside agitator. I said, "I'm Albert Turner, I'm not an outside agitator, I'm the leader here. . . ."

They took me and shoved me into the middle of the crowd. Once they did that, they just started beating the people. After that, we ran trying to get back into the church. A lot of people got in and some didn't.

Once we got into the church some of the troopers tried to get in the church. Once they started into the church we decided it was enough of that. So I had some of my stronger guys line up in a line. . . . If they attempted to come in that church we were all lined up. I gave them some chair rims and backs. We broke the chairs, so they got some sticks in their hands.

Nonviolence was over. We were not going to let them come inside that building. After we got out of the streets and back into that building we were not going [to] let anybody in that building.

That same night, 26-year-old Jimmy Lee Jackson was murdered in Marion by the local police. The police were eager to attack any blacks they found. Jackson was trying to protect his grandfather—who was bleeding—and his mother. The three fled into a building, and the police followed. One of them hit Jackson's mother. Jackson struck back and was shot and killed.

Albert Turner recalled the brutality of Jackson's death in this account:

> Jimmy was murdered that night, and it was known he was murdered for the sole purpose to frighten and push black people back. We decided that because of what happened here that night and [because it was so vicious], that the movement would have to step up. So our tactic was to carry Jimmy Lee Jackson's dead body to Montgomery and drop it on the steps of the capitol. We had really had it. Dr. King said, "No, let's don't do that, but instead, all of us are going to go to Montgomery. That's what started the Selma to Montgomery March. We were really fired up. We were going to win our rights or die. It was the first time the system [in Marion] had outright attacked the people because they were black. If you were a preacher or a teacher, if you were out on the streets that night, they attacked you. It was that simple.

The march from Selma to the state capital of Montgomery was scheduled for March 7. SNCC felt that this march was too dangerous. However, any member could take part in the march if he or she wanted. The first attempt was stopped by a posse of 100 men under the command of Selma's Sheriff Jim Clark and 100 state troopers sent by George Wallace, the governor of Alabama. The state troopers, who were on horses, beat the marchers as they crossed the Edmund Pettus Bridge. They also threw tear gas at the marchers and rode over them when they fell down. Reporters called this ugly violence "Bloody Sunday."

Forced to turn back that day, Dr. King called on everyone—from ministers to movie stars to politicians—to join him in a

Mourners crowd the church as the body of Jimmy Lee Jackson is brought in for funeral services.

second march. And come they did—from all over the country! "When they sicced those dogs, horses, mules, and morons on those people that Sunday, that was an open invitation to the whole world to come to Selma," said Rev. James Anderson.

"Bloody Sunday found me in Atlanta on my way to Alabama," Carmichael said. "We left immediately upon hearing the news and arrived that night." On the way, Carmichael and others learned that Malcolm X, a black leader in New York City, had been killed. Malcolm X was the founder of the Muslim Mosque, Inc. and Organization of Afro-American Unity. Malcolm X had gone to Selma just three weeks before his death. He made a speech there in which he warned whites that if they didn't listen to Martin Luther King, Jr., they would have to deal with people like him. Malcolm X had a reputation for violence. But he never told blacks to be violent. He only encouraged them to defend themselves. He also urged his people to get in touch with their African roots and to be proud of their heritage.

Carmichael had been greatly influenced by Malcolm X. "I resolved to do everything to put his politics in action," he said when he heard about Malcolm X's death. In Selma, Carmichael was one of the speakers at Jimmy Lee Jackson's funeral. In fact, it was at this funeral that he first said the words "black power." Later, he was in the front ranks of the SNCC workers who took part in the Selma to Montgomery march.

On March 10, 1965, a second attempt to march was stopped. Dr. King again turned 1,500 marchers around at the Edmund Pettus Bridge. The marchers didn't have a permit to march, they were told. King didn't want to put them in danger for this reason. He had made an agreement with the local police that the marches would not force a fight. King's action angered many SNCC workers, who felt that he had gone soft on them.

But King might have been wise to avoid violence. That night, Rev. James Reeb, a white minister who took part in the march, was attacked by local whites. He died several days later. Reeb's death drew the attention of the entire country, and his wife received a message of sympathy from President Johnson. Many of the SNCC activists took note of this and thought it was an insult to Jimmy Lee Jackson and the black community. Why did the president respond to the death of a white man but not to the death of a black man? Carmichael spoke up about this:

> Now, I'm not saying we shouldn't pay tribute to Rev. Reeb. What I'm saying is that if we're going to pay tribute to one, we should also pay tribute to the other. And I think we have to analyze why [Johnson] sent flowers to Mrs. Reeb, and not to Mrs. Jackson.

The marchers got their permit. On March 21, 1965, the great march from Selma to Montgomery finally started out. It took five days. Most people marched only part of the way, but there were some who marched the entire 54 miles. Blacks, whites, and people from all walks of life participated. At the end of the march, some 25,000 people walked peacefully into Montgomery. There Dr. King delivered one of his best speeches.

Among the marchers there was great happiness. But white southerners had bitter feelings toward the marchers. On March 25, Viola Liuzzo, a white homemaker from Detroit, was shot to death on the highway between Selma and Montgomery. She had been carrying marchers back to Montgomery in her car.

Even though the march was a success, SNCC workers weren't satisfied. They felt that King was getting in the way of their efforts to build power in the local black communities. Some of the young people were beginning to believe less in nonviolence. Carmichael decided it was time to try his ideas for an all-black political party in another place. He felt that the MFDP was set on "integrating" the Democratic party. To try to make it an independent party would have been too difficult. But it might be possible to form an all-black party by organizing a county in Alabama.

Writer James Baldwin, singer Joan Baez, and civil rights activist James Forman march in Alabama.

The march from Selma to Montgomery had passed right through Lowndes County. Carmichael said he and other SNCC workers "got all the names of local people in Lowndes who came to the march and offered assistance." He said it was these names and the march itself "that gave us our first start in Lowndes."

THE BIRTH OF THE BLACK PANTHERS

> *When a Black man, whose destiny and identity have always been controlled by others, decides and states...he will control his own destiny and rejects the identity given to him by others, he is talking revolution.*

JAMES BALDWIN, writer

Carmichael arrived in Lowndes County on March 26, 1965. All he had was $12 and the name of someone with whom he could stay. Although he was only 24 years old, he was already an activist who knew how to create a mass movement. Lowndes County, Alabama, is between Selma and Montgomery. It was a part of the black belt of the South, a place where more blacks than whites lived. The soil is rich, which makes the county a top area for farming and the paper industry. Most of the people of Lowndes lived in one-story houses that were spread out over the countryside. In 1965, about 15,400 people lived in the county and 80 percent of them were black. In most of the South in 1965, whites had all the power. Lowndes County was no different.

Before SNCC appeared, black leadership in Lowndes County was mostly in the church, and in social and school areas. Such organizations as the Order of the Eastern Star, Elks, and Masons, which were all social or religious groups, had a lot of influence inside the black community, but they had no political power outside of it. Not a single black person there was registered to vote. Not one!

Carmichael and a handful of SNCC workers set out to perform the hard job of organizing and uplifting the people of Lowndes County. Carmichael's title was director for the voting project. He tried to reach the local people on their own terms. To blend in with them, he often wore overalls and a farm hat. He used the local transportation, which was often a mule.

Carmichael was warm and outgoing, and he could speak to the local people in their own way. These qualities helped him to bridge the gap between middle-class blacks and poor blacks. Carmichael felt strongly that middle-class blacks and students from the North should bring their skills to the southern communities to strengthen them. These middle-class blacks and students from the North were usually better educated than the young people and many backs in the South. Some were studying to be lawyers. They had what it took to talk to the people down south and get them together.

The black farmers in Lowndes County often carried guns. They believed in protecting themselves. It was a common practice for whites to threaten a black if he or she were alone— especially on the roads at night. Racism was at its worst in this area of the South. Most blacks felt that if they didn't protect themselves, they might end up dead.

The type of work SNCC did in southern communities was different from that of the SCLC and other civil rights organizations. SNCC workers didn't give speeches to huge crowds urging them to march. They were trying to rally people in the rural South, where no TV cameras followed to see whether whites attacked or killed them. As they visited blacks on lonely farms, SNCC workers had to walk down dark, deserted country roads.

When SNCC members were criticized for carrying weapons, Carmichael said, "We are not King or SCLC. They don't do the kind of work we do nor do they live in the same areas we live in. They don't ride the highways at night."

There were now hundreds of SNCC workers invading the most racist section of the United States. This was very scary to the whites in power. Also, the SNCC teams, at least in the beginning, were made up of both black and white workers. This made the white racists even angrier.

Carmichael was very good at running voter-registration workshops and training young people. Some of this training taught the young people nonviolent tactics. They learned about different laws, and what they should do if bad things happened to them—if they got hit with tear gas or ran into a violent crowd of whites for example.

One of Carmichael's first tasks in Lowndes County was to convince the local blacks that they should vote. These blacks had lived with racism, hatred from whites, fear of "the lynching mob," and economic threats for more than a century. They were afraid to register to vote. In addition, many blacks didn't know how to read or write, and they had to take a test before they could vote. SNCC therefore started classes to teach reading and writing. By August 1965, Carmichael had managed to register 250 people. This wasn't a huge number, but it was a beginning.

On August 6, President Lyndon B. Johnson signed the Voting Rights Act, after six months of protesters' marches and demonstrations. The march from Selma to Montgomery had convinced Congress to pass the act. This act guaranteed blacks their constitutional right to vote. The Voting Rights Act made all literacy tests illegal. The attorney general now had the power to supervise national elections in the South. His representatives could register anyone who wasn't listed. The attorney general could also sue states that required voters to pay poll taxes. The passage of the act helped SNCC right away. A representative from the national government in Washington, D.C., went to Lowndes and declared that the literacy test used there was now against the law.

Jonathan Daniels, a white man who was studying to be a minister, also went to Lowndes County. He worked closely with Carmichael and with many blacks there. Carmichael felt that he was "an honest, unafraid, courageous human [who believed in] human equality . . . and was willing to [give his life] for that cause. I had to tell him, when he first spoke of coming to Lowndes, that I would never approve it because I would be sentencing him to sure death. He was determined. And the SCLC brought him into the county. . . . He [used] to tell me that he thought I valued the life of white people more than Africans, since I knew SNCC people could be killed in Lowndes but I did not want white people killed there." Unfortunately, Carmichael was right. Jonathan Daniels was killed when a deputy sheriff fired into a group of demonstrators. His death made Carmichael very angry.

In spite of Daniels's death, SNCC's work began to pay off. Blacks in Lowndes County began to register to vote in large numbers. But there was more and more white resistance, or "backlash." *White backlash* meant that for every step blacks took toward political growth, whites did whatever they could to tear down those efforts. This backlash might take the form of firing blacks who registered to vote from their jobs or throwing them off the farms they rented from whites. Sometimes blacks and their white supporters were killed. Black voter registration was a big threat to the local whites. Some SNCC workers began to ask certain questions. Does it make sense to get blacks to register? Does it make sense to register them as Democrats? There were no black members of either the Democratic or the Republican party in Lowndes County. Local blacks agreed that they should start a new party.

At this time, Carmichael was reading about the black nationalist philosophy of Malcolm X. A black nationalist is someone who believes that blacks should create their own community—one that is separate and apart from the rest of the United States. Until just before he was killed, Malcolm X believed in separatism. Malcolm X had written that a "black man should control the economy of his community, the politics of his community and so forth. . . ." He changed some of his thinking, but his words of black pride and unity still had meaning for many African Americans.

In the fall of 1965, SNCC and the local blacks of Lowndes County decided to try to control the politics of their community. They formed the Lowndes County Freedom Organization (LCFO). The LCFO wanted to become a real third party, along with the Democratic and Republican parties.

Carmichael said:

> . . . in Alabama my major work was in Lowndes . . . any movement in Selma, Montgomery, Marion, etc., on my part was in relation to trying to get these projects to follow the path of LCFO (the Lowndes County Freedom Organization). SCLC and Martin Luther King., Jr., [did not believe in what] LCFO [stood for]. It was all African and made no appeals to whites. . . . It called for the destruction of the Democratic Party. . . . These were not new platforms to SCLC [and] in no way did they diminish my love, respect, and admiration for Martin Luther King, Jr., and his organization.

In Alabama, an independent party needed 20 percent of the vote in an election in order to be recognized. John Hulett, a member of the Lowndes County Christian Movement for Human Rights, became the chairman of the LCFO. It was Hulett who had invited SNCC to help organize the blacks of Lowndes

County. The LCFO was all black, mostly because whites didn't even try to join it. A snarling black panther was chosen as the symbol for the new independent party. Of this symbol, Hulett said: "[The] panther is a [fierce] animal, as you know. He never bothers anything, but when you start pushing him, he moves backwards, backwards, and backwards into his corner, and then he comes out to destroy everything that's before him. Negroes in Lowndes County have been pushed back through the years. We've [lost] our rights to speak, to move, and to do whatever we want to do at all times. And now we're going to start moving...."

By the time the rest of the county heard of the LCFO, it had been given a nickname. The newspapers called the group the Black Panther Party. The name stuck. During the course of the fall, Carmichael worked with the local people to overcome their own fears of an all-black party. Many believed that something all black was bad. This attitude was part of the brainwashing that blacks had experienced since the beginning of slavery. Carmichael tried to show them that they needed more political power.

There was a clause in the Alabama laws that prevented an independent party from forming if it took part in the Democratic National Convention. For this reason, many blacks boycotted the Democratic primary election to make sure that the LCFO could be legally formed. The entire country heard about Stokely Carmichael when *Look* magazine wrote an article about the Lowndes County project. R. L. Strickland was a black man who lived in the county. He told *Look*, "I just decided that a person had to do something. It's bad to live in fear and abuse. After years of shuffling and saying 'yas, suh,' your senses start rebelling, and your whole mind and body say, 'Man, stand up.'"

As election time drew near, fear and hope filled the air in Lowndes County. By election day, SNCC had been able to register 2,000 blacks. But they hadn't expected the whites in Lowndes County to fight back against the blacks as viciously as they did. More than 20 families were thrown off their farms by white landlords during the voter-registration drives. SNCC responded by setting up tents for the families who had lost their homes. In addition, blacks who lived on plantations were driven to the polls by white landowners who watched them vote. These blacks were afraid not to vote for white candidates.

In the end, the LCFO received less than 46 percent of the votes. The seven blacks who ran under the LCFO were defeated by white candidates. Carmichael had left the project several months before the election, and this might have affected the low number of votes for the LCFO. Only one SNCC organizer, H. Rap Brown, was there full-time. Carmichael returned a few days before the election with more SNCC staff workers. But by that time, his last-ditch efforts to get black voters to the polls just weren't enough.

Even though the LCFO lost the election, blacks in Lowndes County were now better organized. SNCC had shown them that it was possible for them to achieve more political power. Carmichael himself had learned a great deal about putting his political ideas to work. He was eager to take this experience one step further.

After the election in Lowndes County, Carmichael began to think about running for the position of chairman of SNCC. He had grown tired of the nonviolent approach of the current chairman, John Lewis. The more Carmichael worked for black political power, the more he believed in black nationalism. This leaning toward black nationalism was largely a result of what he had learned from Malcolm X. Running for chairman of SNCC was a big step for Stokely Carmichael—a step that would change the rest of his life.

THE NEW CHAIRMAN OF SNCC

❝ Our objective is complete freedom, complete justice, complete equality, by any means necessary. ❞

MALCOLM X

In the middle of May 1966, Carmichael went to a SNCC retreat in Kingston Springs, Tennessee. The main purpose of the retreat was to discuss SNCC projects and to hold SNCC elections. Members could usually tell how the SNCC elections would turn out. The same people often ran for office because no one challenged them. John Lewis had been the chairman of SNCC since 1963. James Forman, one of several older SNCC members, had been the executive secretary since 1961.

Many questions arose at the main meeting. Some of them were: Who should run SNCC? Could SNCC change enough to meet the growing political needs of black people? Many of the younger and more militant activists of SNCC felt that Lewis stood for the old school of the civil rights movement. Lewis was guided mainly by religious beliefs and by the idea of non-violence. He was criticized for going on a European fund-raising tour for SNCC and for attending the planning sessions of the White House Conference on Civil Rights. Some SNCC members didn't like the fact that Lewis also served on the board of the SCLC. SNCC and the SCLC were beginning to move in very different directions. The two groups also had different attitudes toward nonviolence. Lewis had the respect and admiration of many SNCC members, but many of them also thought he was behind the times.

Compared with Lewis, Carmichael was a lively speaker with fire in his words. He was confident and had made a name for himself as a good organizer. He had created a very successful black-power group in Lowndes County. This group had become a model for freedom organizations in the South. Carmichael didn't support Lewis's belief in nonviolence. Lewis refused to even think about having SNCC run only by blacks. It was a standoff.

Carmichael was the first person to run for an office in SNCC. This election was a serious event. Lewis stood for the "old school" of SNCC, and Carmichael stood for the "militant black nationalists." Militant black nationalists believed that blacks should fight for their own separate nation within the United States. This nation of blacks, they believed, should then work toward its own goals apart from the goals of white America.

Militant black nationalists were frightening to many whites and even to some blacks. With Lewis as chairman, SNCC would avoid having to deal with the new militants. But if Carmichael won, SNCC would have to begin paying more attention to them. At first, most of the staff members were in favor of John Lewis, who was reelected chairman. Then a long battle took place. A former SNCC member challenged the election, saying Lewis no longer represented what most SNCC members believed. As a result, the election for the chairman of SNCC was held again. The discussion turned into a five-hour debate. One SNCC member described how the Carmichael and Lewis teams battled it out: "Friends turned upon friends, promises were broken and tears were freely shed."

In the end, Lewis decided to resign in order to make way for the new people. The members elected Carmichael as the new chairman of SNCC. He was 24 years old at the time. Even though Lewis was unhappy about his defeat, he stayed on friendly terms with Carmichael.

Now that SNCC had a new chairman, the organization needed to make it clear what direction it would take. One organizer who had been with SNCC for a long time felt that it should begin working on three levels: (1) SNCC workers should use nationalism as a way to organize the black community; (2) they should begin to build community-wide political movements, such as the LCFO; and (3) white SNCC organizers should begin "to organize the white community around black needs, around black history, the relative importance of blackness in the world today."

At the close of the election, SNCC staff members created a new Central Committee with Carmichael as one of its new members. The Central Committee now replaced the Executive Committee of SNCC and would be responsible for running the organization and deciding what its most important work would be. The committee would also develop new projects and manage the regional offices of SNCC.

Carmichael's supporters included several people with whom he had been close friends while he was a student at Howard University. There was now only one white person on the Central Committee of SNCC. With new people and new goals, SNCC was ready to grow in a new direction.

The newspapers reported on Carmichael's election and wondered what it meant. The *Atlanta Constitution* predicted that under Carmichael's leadership, SNCC would turn toward black nationalism. The *Los Angeles Times* called Carmichael "one of the more radical [extreme] leaders of SNCC."

Through SNCC, Carmichael wanted to bring the Freedom Party setup that he had built in Lowndes County to other areas. He also wanted to build up the staff of SNCC in the South. As chairman of SNCC, Carmichael's job was enormous. He had to pay attention to all the various projects of SNCC. He had to keep track of the many SNCC offices and projects in all regions of the country. He had to make sure SNCC had enough money. He also had to come up with new SNCC programs for the

Stokely Carmichael often wore overalls when out with the people organizing for civil rights.

This was the 1960s headquarters of the Lowndes County Freedom Organization.

entire country. Fortunately, he had the aid of a staff that believed in what they were doing.

Carmichael felt strongly that a black person wanted "to build something of his own, something that he builds with his own hands. And that is *not* anti-white. When you build your own house, it doesn't mean you tear down the house across the street." He felt that blacks needed their own organization in this society. He also felt that action should come not out of hatred for whites but out of a need for blacks to have something they could call their own. There was something Carmichael didn't know, however. Forces larger than he would bring greater changes in the months to come. But for now, Carmichael settled into his new role as chairman of SNCC.

GIVE MORE POWER TO THE PEOPLE!

66 We are the last revolutionaries in America—the last transfusion of freedom into the bloodstream of democracy. Because we are, we must mobilize our wintry discontent to transform the cold heart and white face of this nation. 99

ADAM CLAYTON POWELL, JR.,
clergyman, politician, civil rights
leader

In May 1966, James Meredith announced that he would try to walk across Mississippi to prove that the black people of that state could enjoy their rights without fear. In 1962, Meredith became the first black person to attend the University of Mississippi. Some civil rights leaders thought that Meredith's solo journey across Mississippi was foolish— almost like committing suicide. On June 6, 1966, Meredith was walking along U.S. Highway 51, south of Hernando, Mississippi. Suddenly three shotgun blasts tore through him. He was badly wounded, but he wasn't killed. This was only the second day of his walk.

Civil rights leaders and activists went into an uproar. When Carmichael received word that Meredith had been shot, he rushed to Mississippi. When he arrived Martin Luther King, Jr., Roy Wilkins, the head of the NAACP, and Floyd McKissick, the head of CORE, were already at the scene. Carmichael had planned to be in Mississippi for only a day, but he decided to meet with the other civil rights leaders. They were outraged by the shooting and wanted to discuss plans to continue the march Meredith had begun.

Carmichael was in favor of the march, but other members of SNCC's Central Committee weren't. The committee had to decide whether SNCC should be involved in the march. Carmichael argued that the march could help local voter-registration drives. It could bring attention to towns where blacks still weren't registered. It could also show officials of the federal government where the voting laws weren't being enforced. Carmichael also felt that the march would go to places where SNCC had started projects. These projects were now operating on their own. SNCC would have a chance to see how these projects were doing. He hoped, too, that the media would show just how poorly blacks in Mississippi still lived. Carmichael won, and SNCC's Central Committee agreed to join the march.

Carmichael later met with the other civil rights leaders. He wanted to play down the part that whites played in the march. He also wanted protection for the marchers. This protection came from a Louisiana group call the Deacons for Defense and Justice. The leaders who believed in nonviolence weren't sure this was a good idea because the group practiced self-defense and was well known for being tough. The Deacons for Defense and Justice were allowed to participate, but Dr. King requested that they not carry guns during the march. King felt that if the Deacons brought guns, they might attract violence. That settled, SNCC, the SCLC, and CORE agreed to continue the march across Mississippi together in the name of James Meredith.

The second march across Mississippi was organized within four or five days. There was little time to prepare. It began on June 7, 1966. It started at the exact place where James Meredith had been shot a few days earlier. To the old-timers, this march was like the better days of the march from Selma to Montgomery. There was plenty of attention from the press. Martin Luther King, Jr., hoped the march would speed up passage of the civil rights bill that was pending in Congress.

As the march moved on, the number of marchers changed day by day. First there were a few dozen. Then several hundred more joined the march. Soon there were differences of opinion among the leaders. SCLC thanked northern whites for coming south to join the march. But the SNCC workers wondered whether whites should be in the march at all.

SNCC, the SCLC, and CORE began to disagree in public over their differences. At night there were rallies. These became contests among the leaders of the three organizations. They all wanted the support of the local black people. Carmichael and McKissick felt that blacks needed to be more militant. They felt that the federal government wasn't taking enough action to help southern blacks. Dr. King felt that African Americans should continue to use nonviolent methods of protest.

Carmichael wanted to use the march to gain support for the idea of black power. Willie Ricks, a SNCC activist from Tennessee, was good at getting crowds excited. Before the march, Ricks had used the slogan "black power for black people" at the rallies. Then he shortened the slogan to "black power." Ricks told the Central Committee how much the audiences had liked the term "black power." Carmichael decided to use the words himself.

On June 17, the marchers entered the town of Greenwood, Mississippi. Once there, they tried to set up tents on the grounds of a school. The police told the marchers the school grounds couldn't be used without the school board's permission. Carmichael tried to settle the dispute and ended up in jail for six hours for resisting the police order. That night a rally was held. About 600 people showed up. Carmichael was the last speaker. He was still angry about being arrested. He told the audience, "This is the twenty-seventh time I have been arrested. I ain't going to jail no more." He said blacks had been demanding freedom for six years and had gotten nothing. "What we gonna start saying now is 'black power.' Carmichael shouted the slogan again and again. Each time the audience shouted back, "Black power!" Willie Ricks leapt to the platform and asked, "What do you want?" Again and again the audience shouted out, "Black power!"

The idea of black power was a sign of change for African Americans. Some people called it a publicity trick. But it was an idea that had been passed down from Marcus Garvey many years earlier. Garvey had founded the Universal Negro Improvement Association and begun the back-to-Africa movement. Paul Robeson, the actor and black activist, and Adam Clayton Powell, the U.S. congressman from Harlem, had later used the slogan. Now Willie Ricks and Stokely Carmichael were shouting it. The blacks who lined the road of the march liked it even more than the "freedom now" chant of Dr. King and the SCLC.

Carmichael decided later:

> This country knows what power is and knows it very well. And knows what black power is, because it's deprived black people of it for four hundred years. So it knows what black power is. But the question is, why do white people in this country associate black power with violence? Because of their own inability to deal with blackness. If we had said Negro power, nobody would get scared. Everybody would support it. And if we said power for colored people, every-

body would be for that. But it is the word *black*, it is the word *black* that bothers people in this country, and that's their problem, not mine.

From that moment, there was a big struggle between the "freedom now" people and the "black power" people in the march. Reporters had a free-for-all, quoting Carmichael and trying to figure out what the term "black power" meant. King didn't reject the idea of black power completely, but he felt that it sounded too much like black nationalism and violence. The SCLC, the NAACP, and the Urban League (another civil rights organization) were afraid that Carmichael's cry for black power called for separation of the races and would hurt civil rights efforts.

But "black power" became the chant of the march across Mississippi. Carmichael came forth as the central figure of this march. As the march moved on into Madison, Canton, and Philadelphia, Mississippi, the marchers did indeed run into violence. They met with several mobs of whites, and at one point whites and blacks fired guns at one another.

James Meredith had recovered from his gunshot wounds. He joined the march in a car two miles before it ended on June 26, 1966, at Jackson, Mississippi. At the end of the march, there were about 12,000 to 15,000 marchers present, but many wondered what the march had achieved. For the most part, people across the United States were interested in answering this question: "What is this black power Stokely Carmichael is talking about?"

11 CARMICHAEL LAUNCHES A NEW ERA IN SNCC AND THE NATION

> **66** *We must urge you to fight now to be the leaders of today, not tomorrow. We've got to be the leaders of today.* **99**
>
> **STOKELY CARMICHAEL**

To SNCC, its new chairman stood for the new mood and political hopes of African Americans. According to one historian of the period, "Stokely Carmichael's election was an expression of the hope of SNCC staff members that SNCC could awaken Afro-American political consciousness [awareness] as a [first] step toward building a new social order."

One of Carmichael's first acts as chairman of SNCC was to pull SNCC out of the White House Conference on Civil Rights. The members of SNCC delivered a statement when they left the conference. They said the conference was a way "to shift responsibility for the [low] position in which blacks find themselves away from the oppressor to the oppressed."

Other civil rights groups were alarmed by Carmichael's decision. They accused SNCC of being an isolationist group—a group that wanted to keep blacks separate from whites. The NAACP, the SCLC, and the Urban League began to separate themselves from SNCC, and they made public statements against SNCC. Roy Wilkins, the director of the NAACP, said: "Though it be made clear again and again, 'black power' . . . can mean in the end only black death."

Bayard Rustin, a founder of the SCLC, said: " 'Black power' not only lacks any real value for the civil rights movement, but . . . its [growth] is positively harmful. It diverts the movement from a meaningful debate over strategy and tactics, it isolates the Negro community, and it encourages the growth of anti-Negro forces."

Carl Rowan, an important black reporter, said in *Ebony* magazine: "Isolation is a trap; 'black power' is a phony cry, a plain, old-fashioned [trick]."

Dr. Martin Luther King, Jr., said that the idea of blacks being separate from whites was bad. But even though he didn't agree with SNCC and Carmichael, Dr. King kept working with them. On the other hand, CORE, under the leadership of Floyd McKissick, was one of the biggest supporters of SNCC's new "militancy."

When he first began as chairman, Carmichael planned to make SNCC stronger. However, after the Meredith march across Mississippi in June 1966, Carmichael became known as the architect of black power. Newspapers and magazines attacked him. Answering questions about black power took a lot of time away from his duties as chairman.

Carmichael tried to calm the fears of the whites in the organization who saw him as antiwhite. But he was angry at their reaction to his idea of blacks working separately. Carmichael felt that "one of the most disturbing things about almost all white supporters of the movement had been that they are afraid to go into their own communities—which is where racism exists—and work to get rid of it. They want to run from Berkeley to tell us what to do in Mississippi; let them preach non-violence in the white community." Carmichael spoke sharply about some whites. But he still wanted to keep SNCC as an organization of both blacks and whites. He understood one thing all too well. The whites who were supporters and staff members of SNCC formed a kind of safety shield around SNCC. Their membership prevented white racists from trying to destroy SNCC.

Perhaps the black power slogan had the greatest effect on SNCC itself. When Carmichael first became chairman, and "black power" became SNCC's slogan, the organization began to lose important people. Many of the old-time black activists on the staff left, along with the white staff. SNCC became linked with the black militant movement. As a result, many no longer wanted to be a part of SNCC.

In addition, there were fewer and fewer people to replace the staff who had left. Many of them didn't know how to run the projects SNCC had launched in the South. Many of the offices in Mississippi and Alabama were no longer effective because they had lost contact with SNCC's main office in Atlanta. Many blacks in the cities had begun to join SNCC because of its militant stand, but they weren't interested in the southern projects and did little to support them.

The loss of funds from white supporters also hurt SNCC. Without these funds, it couldn't afford to hire as many full-time workers and many good projects died. Some projects were closed because the staff had no leadership or direction. Soon many SNCC workers found that they just didn't care anymore.

In several cities, SNCC got into fights with the police, who destroyed the organization's property, arrested staff members, and found other ways of harassing them. In August 1966, 80 armed policemen raided the local SNCC office in Philadelphia, Pennsylvania. They said they found dynamite there and arrested many SNCC staff members. SNCC was accused of trying to start a war in the city. The mayor and the chief of police wanted to stop Carmichael from speaking in Philadelphia and other northern cities. Shortly after this, Carmichael was arrested in Atlanta. The police said that he had stirred up a riot. Even though he hadn't been where the riot took place, Carmichael was found guilty of those charges.

More and more, SNCC and other militant groups began to come under attack from the federal government. City police were ordered to follow members around and break up their meetings. The media began to report false information about Carmichael and SNCC. The FBI began to watch Carmichael.

Carmichael was constantly having to clear up the mistaken ideas the media spread about black power. But he had little power to fight back against the picture the newspapers, radio, and TV were creating. The media were against him and SNCC. They played up to the fears of the whites, who now felt that they should fight back against black power.

Carmichael had now become more of a media person and speaker for black power. As a result, he was doing less of his real work of organizing for SNCC. Key members of SNCC's Central Committee began to resent Carmichael and to believe that he was bad for SNCC. SNCC was developing fewer and fewer projects now, and there was very little money. Some committee members thought this was Carmichael's fault. Some of the whites who had given money to SNCC wrote angry letters. "When you talk about 'white America,' you are talking about me too.... And I have a strong prejudice against being bad-mouthed with my own money," wrote one supporter. Another one wrote: "I am a white liberal.... My purpose in writing you is to tell you bluntly to take my name off your mailing list. I want no part of SNCC."

SNCC turned its attention to organizing some of the northern cities, but the blacks there weren't interested. Many of the SNCC staff found that they couldn't work in the cities in the same way they had worked in the farmlands of the South, so they had little success. Shifting staff people from the South to the North had a harmful effect on the southern projects, which were already failing.

At the end-of-the-year staff meeting of SNCC in December 1966, black power was discussed. The staff members who made up the Atlanta Project wanted racial separatism. They felt that SNCC should no longer have any white staff members. Whites were "the biggest obstacle" in "black folks getting liberation," they said. They wanted SNCC to be a black nationalist organization that set up programs in the black community that were run by blacks only. Carmichael agreed, although he believed SNCC needed whites as a safety net. The issue of separatism divided the SNCC members.

For several days, the SNCC staff discussed the issue of whether whites should be part of the organization. At one point, James Forman got upset over the endless talking. He proposed that they break up SNCC and send the funds it had left to the African liberation movements. He became angry when a few black separatists made fun of old-time staff member Fannie Lou Hamer. She was against removing the whites from the organization. The separatists said Hamer no longer gave meaning to the cause and that she wasn't at their level of development. To them, Hamer's bravery and hard work in the Mississippi Freedom Democratic Party now counted for nothing.

In the end, a resolution to exclude whites was passed. The vote was 19 for and 18 against expelling them. Twenty-four white members didn't vote. They walked out of the meeting after the voting took place. Many of the staff members—both black and white—had mixed feelings of guilt and relief. SNCC had turned a corner, and there was no looking back. Some SNCC members—including the white staff—knew that sooner or later, they would have been expelled. Separation of the races would be an issue in SNCC for several months to come. However, this meeting didn't deal with the problems that had been caused by the storm over the black power slogan. Neither did it deal with the problems and differences that now raged within SNCC.

WHAT IS BLACK POWER?

> **To demand ... God-given human rights is to seek black power—what I call [daring] power; the power to build black institutions of splendid achievement.**
>
> ADAM CLAYTON POWELL, JR.

> **Say it loud, I'm Black and I'm proud.**
>
> JAMES BROWN, entertainer

The black power slogan had an electrifying effect on blacks all over the United States. It spoke to a deep need in the black community—the need for power. Except for the church, blacks had very few examples of black power in their daily lives. James Forman, the former SNCC executive secretary, felt that "only power could change our condition."

The question was: What type of black power was needed? Forman felt that the challenge of black power "was a higher one than 'One Man, One Vote' or 'Freedom Now.' We had moved to the level of [talking about our desire] for power—not merely for the vote, not for some vague kind of freedom, not for legal rights, but the basic force in any society—power. Power for black people, black power."

In the the mid to late 1960s, in the South, black power began to have meaning for African Americans all across the United States. Change wasn't coming as quickly as it should have come.

Lowndes County became an important location for support of black power and the Black Panthers.

Civil rights and new voting laws had been passed by Congress to end discrimination and segregation. But the new political rights of blacks in the South weren't being recognized by whites in many ways. Votes were being counted incorrectly. White racists were bribing and threatening voters. All the old evils of racism were still there. Terrible housing, lack of jobs, not enough medical attention, inferior education—all these things remained basically unchanged throughout black communities, whether in New York or in Mississippi. Black power could change the lives of black people across the nation. "It had emerged from the Southern experience, but had meaning for black people everywhere," said James Forman.

In some circles, the term *black power* came to be used more than the phrase *civil rights movement.* Black power stood for the desire to form organizations and groups that were all black. This was clear as SNCC and other militant groups began to exclude whites from their organizations. Blacks wanted to act in ways that reflected black power and their new sense of black pride. As a result, many black Americans became interested in learning more about Africa, and even made trips to Africa.

The black power slogan was frightening to many white Americans and to the U.S. government because they thought it meant revolution—the kind of change that might threaten or even overthrow the government. Just the idea of blacks united for power scared many white Americans, especially those in the government. Most of the media connected black power with violence. They decribed black power as being against the "American way," which to them meant the way of slow and orderly change.

Stokely Carmichael was now being betrayed by the very same media that had cheered his work in Lowndes County, Alabama, a little more than a year earlier. Carmichael took the brunt, or weight, of the negative fears the term "black power" aroused in people. Reporters and writers described Carmichael as someone who took advantage of things, as someone who wanted to work alone, as someone who wasn't responsible.

Olympic medal winners (1968) show their support of black power in the United States with this gesture.

More than 20 years later, Carmichael would be unable to overcome this impression that Americans had of him.

In 1967, a year after he had been elected chairman of SNCC, Carmichael and Charles V. Hamilton wrote a book called *Black Power: The Politics of Liberation in America*. Carmichael gave all the money he made on the book to SNCC. It was "very important that an example be set," he said. "My mother was unemployed but I gave the money to SNCC, knowing in this way I would help more mothers."

In *Black Power*, Carmichael discussed how the lack of black power had affected several projects in which he was involved. He and Hamilton discussed how the Mississippi Freedom Democratic Party and the Lowndes County Freedom Organization came about. They told why they thought these organizations were successful and where they had fallen short. They felt that perhaps they had fallen short because they could somehow have gotten more blacks to come forth and vote. Some of the problems of blacks living in ghettos were examined, such as the lack of good housing and jobs. The book also discussed possible solutions for blacks in America. It questioned the need for different political groups to work together. And it took a hard look at President Lyndon B. Johnson's War on Poverty program, which was supposed to help poor blacks and whites. Why, Carmichael asked, were there no African Americans at the decision-making level in the War on Poverty? Why didn't the War on Poverty deal with black Americans quickly and directly, the way SNCC had in the Lowndes County project? The War on Poverty tried to lift all Americans out of poverty through major reform measures: the Civil Rights Act of 1964, the Equal Opportunity Act of 1964, and a personal income tax cut. Carmichael and Hamilton both felt that these measures weren't enough. They believed that whites had to deal with problems in the black community. If they didn't, the United States would become a time bomb that could explode.

In *Black Power,* Carmichael defined the idea of black power as "a call for black people in this country to unite, to recognize their heritage, to build a sense of community.... The concept of Black Power rests on a fundamental premise: *Before a group can enter the open society, it must first close ranks.* By this we mean that group [unity] is necessary before a group can operate effectively from a bargaining position of strength in a pluralistic [or mixed] society."

During his year as chairman of SNCC, Carmichael made black power a national issue for blacks as well as whites. Some people felt that SNCC had made a mistake. They should have set up programs to deal with the issues around black power. This would have allowed Carmichael and others a chance to control what was said and thought about the idea. Carmichael failed to develop a clear-cut program for black power. But he did give African Americans pride and strength by making the concept of black power irresistible to them. Black power gave a lift to black pride. Young blacks even made up a black power salute that was a greeting. It was a clenched fist lifted up above the head.

The impact of the black power salute was so strong that it created a huge uproar at the 1968 Olympics. Two blacks who won medals for track and field events used the black power salute during the Olympics awards ceremony. U.S. officials criticized them and took away their awards.

African Americans also created a separate flag, using the colors red, black, and green. The red stood for the blood that had been shed by so many blacks in the United States. The black was the color of the people, and the green was a symbol of hope and new life. Many blacks replaced the American flag on the walls of their homes with the black power flag. Many black soldiers fighting in Vietnam hung the red-black-and-green flag in their barracks. There was the Afro hairstyle, which celebrated black hair in its natural, unstraightened state. There were clothes—such as African shirts called dashikis—that became a statement of black people's awareness of their African-American heritage. The symbols of black power were everywhere.

FROM BLACK POWER TO BLACK LIBERATION

" Today, power is international, real power is international; today, real power is not local. The only kind of power that can help you and me is international power, not local power.... If your power base is only here, [in the United States], you can forget it. "

MALCOLM X

In January 1967, Carmichael was trying to rebuild projects that SNCC had started in the South. As part of this work, he began to visit black colleges in the South. SNCC had often found workers at these colleges in the past. Carmichael found that the black students responded to him.

His message of black power made them want to become activists. Carmichael told the students to take a bigger part in the colleges they attended. Colleges across the United States had been under attack from black groups. SNCC and other groups wanted a change in the entrance requirements that kept many blacks out of these colleges. They also wanted black studies programs added to the curriculum. Student members of SNCC were often punished by their colleges for their activities. This treatment usually made them more militant, which in turn gave SNCC a worse reputation for making trouble.

The FBI began to watch SNCC in 1960. By early 1967, the group was being watched more closely. Several SNCC projects even had FBI spies working in them. During the summer of 1967, SNCC was officially added to the list of the FBI's counterintelligence program known as COINTELPRO. COINTELPRO's job was to destroy and discredit black organizations that had been called militant, Communist, or revolutionary. This was done by using spies and stirring up fights among the different groups. Members of militant organizations were often attacked or arrested by the police. Their meeting places were sometimes bombed or set on fire. COINTELPRO watched many militant black organizations during the 1960s.

Stokely Carmichael was on a speaking tour in Nashville, Tennessee, when he was accused of turning a demonstration into a riot. He had spoken at Vanderbilt University in Nashville during a three-day black power gathering. Several hours after he left the university, a demonstration of several hundred people turned into a riot. Carmichael and several SNCC staff members were accused of starting the riot. The mayor of Nashville blamed Carmichael for the violence. The president of the all-black Fisk University accused SNCC's "outside agitators" with starting the violence. The Tennessee House of Representatives quickly adopted a resolution asking that Carmichael be deported, or sent out of the country. Violent events continued to follow Carmichael as he spoke in city after city. Even before this

Stokely Carmichael speaking for black power and against the Vietnam War.

incident in Nashville, he was often mentioned in Congress when a bill was being proposed that would help to prevent riots.

In the law books, the civil rights of blacks might have improved, but the way poor blacks lived hadn't changed very much. As there was more and more talk of black power in the black community, there were also many ways in which this idea was expressed. That expression often took the form of anger that exploded into riots. Gone were the days of the peaceful demonstrations of the early civil rights movement. Terrible riots took place in hundreds of cities across the United States during 1966 and 1967. The anger that black people had kept inside them for so long had finally exploded.

The civil rights movement had given birth to many other

movements—from the fight against the war in Vietnam to equal rights for women. Across the nation, young whites were also taking part in demonstrations and riots. It was a time to challenge the way in which many things were done. Many demonstrations were held to protest the war in Vietnam. There were many conflicts between students and the people in charge of the universities. The militant stand of blacks also inspired other racial and ethnic groups in the United States, such as the Hispanic population, to challenge things.

The black power movement inspired black and Third World countries around the world. The term *Third World* is used to refer to those countries whose industry is not as highly developed as the more advanced countries. The countries included in this term are in Africa, Asia, and Latin America. Most of the people who live in these countries are not white. Many Third World countries were just gaining their independence during the 1960s. They saw how banding together as the blacks in the United States had done could get them more freedom and better jobs in their own countries. They looked to Carmichael and SNCC as the leaders of the black revolution.

Months of racial violence went on in the name of black power. SNCC was attacked more and more by the media, the FBI, and other civil rights groups. Finally, Carmichael decided that he had had enough. He resigned from SNCC in May 1967.

H. Rap Brown, the new SNCC chairman, was even more militant than Carmichael had been. Brown had been a staff member of the Lowndes County Freedom Organization. SNCC members had thought Brown would smooth over the uproar created by Carmichael's black power slogan. Instead, he held a demonstration that ended with the death of four students in Orangeburg, South Carolina. After several days of trying to integrate a bowling alley in Orangeburg, students held a rally at the campus of the University of South Carolina. Cleveland Sellers and H. Rap Brown took part in it. The National Guard said they were fired upon, and they began to shoot at the defenseless

Rep. Adam Clayton Powell of Harlem (right) and E. D. Nixon, former head of the Montgomery NAACP.

students. Four students were killed, 30 were jailed, and 33 were shot. Cleveland Sellers was put into jail for starting a riot, for arson (starting a fire), and for intent to kill. This event came to be known as the Orangeburg Massacre.

A more "mainstream" kind of supporter of black power was Adam Clayton Powell, a black congressman from New York City. In October 1966, Powell held a black power conference, in Newark, New Jersey. Several organizations such as CORE, the Urban League, and the NAACP attended. SNCC and Carmichael played only small parts in this conference. Perhaps this conference showed that black power had become a part of the program of every black organization. In this sense, SNCC was no longer at the center of the black power movement.

SNCC was beginning to be known on a worldwide basis. The Third World nations, especially Communist and Socialist countries, were interested in the group. During 1966 and 1967,

The Long Hot Summers

During the summers of 1965, 1966 and 1967, African Americans began to protest violently against racism in the United States. During those summers, race riots rocked over 100 cities. Riots in Los Angeles, Newark, Detroit, and Chicago told the country that there was racism in the North, East, and West, as well as in the South. Armed soldiers—and sometimes tanks—were sent in to put down the rioting.

President Lyndon B. Johnson soon created a government group to investigate the causes of the riots. This group, called the Kerner Commission, presented its report in 1968. The report said the basic cause of the racial violence was "white racism." The report warned that "our Nation is moving toward two societies, one black, one white—separate and unequal."

Troops patrol the streets of Detroit after rioting in 1967.

Flames rip through a building during the Newark, New Jersey, riots in July 1967.

SNCC staff members were invited to visit North Vietnam, Cuba, the Dominican Republic, the Soviet Union, and Japan.

SNCC activists decided to accept invitations from abroad to deepen their understanding of revolutionary struggle throughout the world. Staff members hoped to see firsthand how revolutions had really worked in the Third World. But they soon discovered that they had difficulty applying communist and socialist ideas to the lives of African Americans in the United States. SNCC began to lose more members. Many people didn't agree with H. Rap Brown's militant position. Others didn't like the idea of SNCC associating with Communist countries.

After stepping down as the chairman of SNCC, Carmichael looked forward to getting together with other groups. For the most part, however, he wanted to get back to his first love—organizing.

Carmichael (left) with SNCC leader H. Rap Brown, who took a militant stand on civil rights.

14 CARMICHAEL GOES ABROAD

> **“** *We are Africans wherever we are.* **”**
>
> **STOKELY CARMICHAEL**

After Stokely Carmichael resigned as chairman of SNCC, he discovered that he was in even greater demand as a speaker at colleges and universities across the United States. Several invitations to speak also came from other countries. However, in spite of the demands of speaking and traveling around the country, he decided to continue his connection with SNCC as an organizer.

SNCC sent Carmichael to San Juan to help the Puerto Rican nationalists there. The Puerto Rican nationalists wanted Puerto Rico to become free of U.S. domination. They were trying to bring their cause to the United Nations. SNCC organizers also went to Albuquerque, New Mexico, to sign a treaty with the Hopi Indians. The Hopi wanted the land of their ancestors to be returned to them.

Carmichael then traveled to Great Britain. In July 1967, he was invited to speak at the Congress of Dialectics of Liberation. In his address to that organization, he said:

> I'm amazed when I pick up the paper and read that "England today decided to give independence to the West Indies." The whole West feels it has the right to *give* everybody their independence. . . . All they can do is stop oppressing me, get off my back. . . . You cannot grant anybody independence, they just take it; and that is what white America is going to learn. No white liberal can give me anything. The only thing a white liberal can do for me is help civilize other whites, because they need to be civilized.
>
> For the past four hundred years the African-American has tried to coexist peacefully inside the United States. . . . We have never lynched a white man, we have never burned their churches, we have never bombed their houses, we have never beaten them in the streets. We have been lynched, our houses have been bombed and our churches burned. Now we are being shot down like dogs in the streets by white racist policemen. We can no longer accept this oppression. . . We understand that as we expand our resistance and internationalize the consciousness of our people we will get retaliation from the government.

Carmichael also said:

> We are not any longer going to bow our heads to any white man. If he touches one black man in the United States, he is going to go to war with every black man in the United States.

Carmichael stirred up the black youth of Great Britain so much that the country placed a ban on him. That is, he was forbidden to return to Great Britain. This ban was effective in more than 30 countries that were part of the British Commonwealth, including Carmichael's place of birth—Trinidad. Because of threats on his life, supposedly by the British police and security services, Carmichael was forced to leave Great Britain in a hurry. Shortly after he left Great Britain, the United Colored Peoples Association was founded to deal with the problems of blacks there.

For Carmichael, this was the beginning of a five-month tour of Communist and Third World countries. This tour received a lot of attention in the media. Carmichael hadn't planned any of this, but one thing led to another as he received invitations to speak all over the world. Carmichael wanted to tell the rest of the world about African Americans and SNCC. However, SNCC didn't like the idea of his traveling so much. The leaders of SNCC felt that Carmichael was traveling overseas for his own benefit rather than in the interest of SNCC.

Perhaps the most talked-about trip Carmichael made was to Havana, Cuba, where he attended a conference of the Organization of Latin-American Solidarity. This visit caused the U.S. government to watch him even more closely because Cuba was an enemy of the United States.

During an interview with a Cuban newspaper, Carmichael said that blacks were "preparing groups of fighters for their defense in cities. At another point, he said, "Afro-Americans in the U.S. are fighting for their liberation . . . It is a . . . total revolution . . . Ours is a struggle for justice, equality and the redistribution of wealth within the U.S." What Carmichael meant by this was that African Americans in the United States were all set to go into the streets and wage war for justice, equal rights, and a share of the wealth of the land. He believed that blacks in the United States formed a colony of people who had been put down for a long time and needed to be set free.

After some U.S. newspapers wrote about what Carmichael said, Congress called for his arrest. He was charged with treason and sedition, or not being loyal to the United States and urging people to break the law. The call to put Carmichael into prison was so strong that Fidel Castro, the president of Cuba, offered to let him stay in Cuba. He said that Cuba would give Carmichael financial support. Carmichael did not accept this offer.

After Cuba, Carmichael went to give a speech in Paris. He was also invited to other countries in Europe and Africa—including Tanzania, Egypt, Algeria, Spain, Guinea, and Czechoslovakia. Everywhere he went, he spoke out against the treatment of blacks in the United States. He called for a total revolution of the black masses. Carmichael wanted to identify the struggle of blacks in the United States with the stuggle of oppressed people around the world.

Perhaps goaded by Carmichael, Congress tried to pass a certain bill. This bill would bring criminal charges against any U.S. citizen who traveled to certain areas of the world. These countries were usually run by governments whose views the United States didn't share. Congress also debated passing several other laws that would punish anyone who called for the overthrow of the government or was guilty of treason and sedition. In fact, one bill was introduced as the Stokely Carmichael bill. Congress kept trying to find a way to put Carmichael on trial for treason. He responded by saying that he "never asked anyone's permission to go anywhere, at any time, for any reason."

During this time, Carmichael met and visited with several important leaders of the Third World. In addition to Fidel Castro, he met Shirley Graham Du Bois, who organized the first five Pan-African conferences. The Pan-African conferences were of major importance because they brought African people from all over the world together. Du Bois's husband was W. E. B. Du Bois, who had started the NAACP in 1909. They were among the first Pan-Africanists in the United

States. W. E. B. Du Bois later settled in Ghana, where he became friends with the exiled leader of Ghana, Kwame Nkrumah. Carmichael met Nkrumah when he was there. He also met President Sékou Touré of the Revolutionary Republic of Guinea. He was called the father of African nationalism.

While Carmichael was in Guinea, President Sékou Touré offered him political asylum. In other words, he was invited to leave the United States and live in Guinea, where he would no longer have to worry about his safety. Dr. Kwame Nkrumah asked Carmichael if he would like to become his personal secretary. During Carmichael's private talks with Touré and Nkrumah, the seeds of Pan-Africanism were firmly planted in him. Nkrumah taught Carmichael that Pan-Africanism was the most important goal to be achieved by blacks. Carmichael soon came to agree with him.

Carmichael also went to the Eighth Congress of the Government of Guinea. This trip to Guinea had the strongest impact on him. While in Guinea, he met South African singer and freedom fighter Miriam Makeba. Makeba had left South Africa in the 1960s. Harry Belafonte, also a famous singer, helped her come to the United States. Makeba had a strong reputation around the world. She became known in the United States for her South African songs. She was also one of the first women to make the Afro hairstyle popular in the United States.

Makeba later spoke out at the General Assembly of the United Nations. There she protested against the crimes of the South African government toward the blacks there. After this, South Africa placed a ban on her, and she came to live in the United States. Makeba was a close friend of Sékou Touré, and she attended the conference as his guest. Later, when Carmichael returned to the United States, Makeba and he began to date. They were married in March 1966. Their marriage represented the coming together of two groups of people who had been separated and oppressed.

From Guinea, Carmichael traveled to North Vietnam. While

in North Vietnam, he met the leader of the country, Ho Chi Minh. Minh also told Carmichael that he should study Pan-Africanism. Minh had met Marcus Garvey, the founder of the back-to-Africa movement, during the 1930s. He felt that African Americans needed a home base in Africa. From that home base, they would be able to connect with Africans around the world. Ho Chi Minh caused Carmichael to think: Why not return to Africa, the true home of African Americans?

Carmichael went back to the United States on December 12, 1967. At Kennedy Airport in New York, his passport was seized by a U.S. marshal. This was done because Carmichael had traveled to Communist countries without getting permission from the U.S. government. This was the only way in which the government could punish him. Without his passport, Carmichael would not be able to leave the United States even to visit an approved country.

From this point, the FBI followed Carmichael wherever he went. According to some accounts, they also listened to what he said on the telephone and fed lies about him to the newspapers to give black organizations the wrong idea about him. The FBI bothered Carmichael's family, too. His mother was followed constantly, and she received calls at all hours of the day and night asking where her son was. His sisters weren't spared either.

Carmichael's travels didn't do him much good at SNCC. His influence there began to slip. Members of SNCC didn't agree with him about Pan-Africanism. All the same, Carmichael continued to work for SNCC.

SNCC was now working with a group called the Black Panther Party for Self-Defense (BPP). Huey P. Newton, the minister of defense, and Bobby Seale, the chairman, set up the BPP in October 1966. The BPP had its base in California. The BPP took the "Panther" in its name from the Lowndes County Freedom Organization. The LCFO had used the symbol of the black panther. The BPP was established to fight police brutality. In Oakland, Los Angeles, and San Francisco, the police were involved in many incidents in which blacks were beaten or killed.

The BPP said that blacks should arm themselves for self-defense. They had armed patrols in California. They soon became famous. The Black Panthers usually arrived at the scene of an arrest in uniforms of black French-style berets, pants, and leather jackets. They carried pistols strapped to their sides, shotguns, rifles, and law books in their hands. The police, as well as many whites, were afraid of the Black Panthers. Because the BPP took a stand against the police and were willing to fight back, young blacks across the nation were attracted to BPP. The BPP had a 10-point program. These 10 points were:

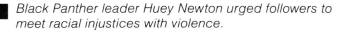

Black Panther leader Huey Newton urged followers to meet racial injustices with violence.

WHAT WE WANT

1. We want freedom. We want power to determine the destiny of our black community.

2. We want full employment for our people.

3. We want an end to the robbery by the white man of our black community.

4. We want decent housing, fit for shelter of human beings.

5. We want education for our people that exposes the true nature of this decadent American society. . . .

6. We want all black men to be exempt from military service.

7. We want an immediate end to police brutality and murder of black people.

8. We want freedom for all black men held in federal, state, county and city prisons and jails.

9. We want all black people when brought to trial be tried in court by a jury of their peer group or people from their black communities, as defined by the Constitution of the United States.

10. We want land, bread, housing, education, clothing, justice and peace. And as our major political objective, a United Nations-supervised [vote] to be held throughout the black colony in which only black colonial subjects will be allowed to participate, for the purpose of determining the will of black people as to their national destiny.

When Carmichael first became chairman of SNCC, he was asked to join the BPP. One member of the BPP remembered that "When we [first] called Stokely and told him that he had been drafted by the Party into our army of black liberation, he had said, 'You can't draft me, I enlist.'"

In 1967, Huey Newton was arrested. He was accused of shooting a policeman to death. While he was awaiting trial, the Panthers couldn't do anything. They came together to form a "free Huey" plan to raise money for his defense and to make the public aware of his case. Shortly after Carmichael returned from his world tour, the BPP asked him to speak at their first Free Huey rally. Carmichael agreed, along with several other SNCC members. James Forman also spoke at the rally, as well as H. Rap Brown. The Free Huey rally was a big success. It raised at least $10,000 for the defense team.

The BPP felt that Carmichael had the type of image they wanted. Forman and Carmichael were invited to join SNCC with the BPP. After the rally, Carmichael was made honorary prime minister of the BPP. James Forman was made minister of foreign affairs, and H. Rap Brown was made minister of justice. SNCC's Central Committee hadn't approved of the two groups coming together. But in spite of this, Carmichael and Forman went ahead with their plans.

In August 1968, Carmichael was expelled from SNCC. SNCC's Central Committee felt that he no longer stood for what they believed. Within three months, SNCC had cut itself off completely from the BPP. Brown and Forman also resigned from the BPP. Carmichael was the only one to remain.

On April 4, 1968, Dr. Martin Luther King, Jr., was assassinated in Memphis, Tennessee. Stokely Carmichael was in Washington at the time. He was shocked and saddened by the news of Dr. King's death. He didn't always agree with King about political issues, but he did understand and respect King's importance to the black struggle. He had thought of King as his friend. Carmichael warned white America "that it had made a mistake by killing King." He said King was "the one man of our race that this country's older generations, the militants and the revolutionaries and the masses of black people would still listen to." People wondered whether Carmichael would try to fill the gap left by the loss of King. King's death left Carmichael feeling lost and angry. But it was a clear sign to him that he, too, might be killed.

Carmichael predicted that violent outbreaks would erupt all over the United States as a result of King's death. He also said

This girl is being arrested during the Washington riots that followed Martin Luther King's murder.

that many blacks would be killed. Martin Luther King, Jr., who believed in nonviolence, had been killed through violence. Like many African Americans, Carmichael felt that with King's death, a mass movement had suddenly halted in its tracks. But the stillness didn't last long. Later, on the same day on which King was murdered, African Americans took to the streets, rioting and looting in many major cities of the United States.

In Washington, D.C., Carmichael went to local neighborhoods asking store owners to close in respect to Dr. King. In spite of this, the rioting and looting continued. The war cry on the streets of America was "Burn, baby burn!" In Washington, Carmichael was blamed for the riots even though the anger of the black mobs couldn't be controlled by anyone. The riots continued for several months after Dr. King's death. Some 20,000 black Americans were arrested and at least 40 were killed during this time.

The BPP came under attack from the government. Several leaders of the Black Panthers were jailed. The U.S. government's treatment of the BPP was so severe that Bobby Seale was chained and gagged while he was in court.

In the meantime, the FBI continued to harass Carmichael and his wife, Miriam Makeba. Makeba began to lose singing jobs in the United States and Europe because she was Carmichael's wife. Carmichael himself began to feel that he had been watched and followed during his entire life. Finally, he and his wife decided to accept Sékou Touré's offer to move to Guinea.

Carmichael had become increasingly dissatisfied with the BPP. As a leader, he had very little to do except act as a spokesperson for the party. Even in this role, however, Carmichael helped to form more than 28 chapters of the BPP across the country.

When Carmichael announced his plans to leave the United States, he was accused of selling out the black power movement and running away. He left the country amid harsh criticism of his activities by both blacks and whites. He felt that he had to spend more time studying and thinking about the political situation of blacks in the world. He also believed that "tactics had to change: the situation now calls for serious, quiet organization. Anybody who does not [follow] this will be wiped out. One of the beautiful things about revolution is the ability to change quickly when change is demanded." He prepared to leave the United States.

Just before the couple left for Africa in 1969, Carmichael helped to establish the first branch of the All African Peoples Revolutionary Party (AAPRP) in Washington, D.C. "The purpose of the All African Peoples Revolutionary Party is to organize the Black man all over the world to channel our [energy] toward the same objective," he said. The AAPRP felt that blacks needed to strive for Pan-Africanism. They believed that Pan-Africanism would lead to total freedom for Africans everywhere.

Carmichael had also accepted Dr. Kwame Nkrumah's invitation to become part of the first AAPRP work-study circle in Conakry, Guinea, along with 15 other young people from around the world. Nkrumah had formed the All African Peoples Revolutionary Party there in 1968. "Pan-Africanism is grounded in the belief that all African peoples, wherever we may be, are one," he said.

Carmichael later said: "Africans today, [regardless] of geographical location, have a common enemy and face common problems. We are victims of imperialism, racism, and we are a landless people."

Carmichael settled in Conakry, Guinea. There he became more determined to use his experience for the liberation of African peoples. He continued to work with the AAPRP that had been established in the United States. Kwame Nkrumah and Sékou Touré became his friends. Carmichael looked up to these men. He also began to take French classes at the French Institute in Guinea. He had become part of a long line of Pan-Africanists inside and outside of Africa. That line included W. E. B. Du Bois, Henry Sylvester Williams, George Padmore, Marcus Garvey, Patrice Lumumba, Malcolm X, Ben Bella, President Sékou Touré, and President Kwame Nkrumah. Carmichael's new ideas developed and blossomed in Conakry. It was a year before Carmichael returned to the United States.

By the age of 28, Stokely Carmichael had become a major political force in the United States. The civil rights movement and the black liberation movement in which he had participated with thousands of people became a beacon—a bright light for people all over the world.

THE QUIET AFTER THE STORM

> **Forward ever, Backward never!**
>
> **KWAME NKRUMAH**

> **Revolution is not a speed race, it is a race for he who runs to the end of his life, it is not a race for racehorses, it is a race for warhorses.**
>
> **STOKELY CARMICHAEL**

In 1969, while in Africa, Carmichael left the Black Panther Party. He didn't believe the BPP should work with whites at all. He thought they would defeat the group's goals in the end. Members of the BPP had also threatened Carmichael several times.

While in Africa, Carmichael studied with President Sékou Touré and Dr. Kwame Nkrumah. After a year in Guinea, Carmichael returned to the United States. In March 1970, he appeared before the Subcommittee to Investigate the Administration of the Internal Security Act and Other Internal Security Laws. This was a very tense time for Carmichael. He was asked to give Congress information on organizations and people that might be planning to overthrow the U.S. government. The congressmen asked him about the Communist party, the Black Panther Party for Self-Defense, and SNCC. They asked him questions about things he had said and done when he was away from the United States. Carmichael pleaded the Fifth Amendment all through this hearing. The Fifth Amendment is the part of the Constitution that says you don't have to answer any questions if you think the answers will get you into trouble. Once the ordeal was over, Congress left Carmichael alone. Soon afterward, he returned to Africa.

In 1971, Carmichael wrote another book called *Stokely Speaks: Black Power Back to Pan-Africanism*. The book contains speeches that cover six years of his work in the civil rights and the black power movements. From the Mississippi Delta to Conkary, Guinea, Carmichael shed light on the struggles of African Americans in the United States as well as Africans in Africa. That same year, SNCC disbanded. The organization Carmichael had hoped would be able to help change conditions in the United States had tried to reorganize but failed.

The year 1978 was a turning point in Carmichael's life. He and his wife, Miriam Makeba, decided to separate. Their 10-year marriage came to an end. Carmichael later married a Guinean woman, Malyatou. Later, they had one son.

In 1978, Stokely Carmichael also changed his name to Kwame Ture in honor of the two men who had most influenced him—Sékou Touré and Kwame Nkrumah. Carmichael saw his name change as a way of cutting off the past that had bound him to a heritage of slavery for so many years.

Kwame Ture spent the next 10 years traveling around the world organizing young people. He was active in the All African Peoples Revolutionary Party, which formed chapters throughout the world. He made good on his promise to

Kwame Ture talking with children in church in Mississippi in 1984.

Nkrumah. He had promised to help the AAPRP grow so that it could spread the word of Pan-Africanism. Nkrumah believed in organizing and politically educating young people around the world. They would then spread Pan-Africanism. The AAPRP's goal has been to build Africa into a unified Socialist country. The AAPRP has described itself in this way:

> We are a revolutionary party. Revolution is made by three sectors, the workers, the peasants [the uneducated people who work on the land] and the revolutionary intelligentsia [the educated people].
>
> At this point . . . we concentrate on the intelligentsia trying to bring them forward to live up to their responsibilities of politically educating the masses of our people. . . .

> We see our major task as the task of organizing our peo-
> ple...in order to organize our people they must be
> politically educated. Our primary task at this time is the
> political education of the masses of our people.

In the United States, the AAPRP organized an African Liberation Day as a national event. Dr. Kwame Nkrumah had
started the celebration of African Freedom Day, April 15, 1958,
in Accra, Ghana. Nkrumah's themes for the conference were
"Hands off Africa" and "Africa must be free." African Freedom
Day was later changed to African Liberation Day. Soon African
Liberation Day was being celebrated on a worldwide basis. On
that day, liberation movements throughout Africa celebrate together. The day is used to "politically educate people about the
struggle for liberation still raging in Africa and to collect money
and supplies for [fighters] and for the millions of refugees."
This major event has usually taken place in Washington, D.C.,
in May. Kwame Ture attended the African Liberation Day fes-
tival in Washington as often as he could.

In 1982, the ban on Kwame Ture was removed in most of the
countries of the British Commonwealth. He spoke there again
in 1983, and the ban went into effect again. A British official,
Leon Brittan, claimed that Ture told black lawyers to go to
Brixton and throw bombs. In 1985, he returned to Trinidad for
the first time in more than 20 years.

"Black power," the slogan that Stokely Carmichael had made
famous, made its mark in the United States, expecially in politics. After the Voting Rights Act of 1965 was passed, thousands
of blacks registered to vote. Over the next 10 years, they voted
many white racist politicians out of office. City politicians such
as Eugene "Bull" Connor, who was in charge of the police in
Birmingham, Alabama, were the first to go. Change occurred
more slowly on the state level. Many racist governors and sena-
tors remained in office for years. But even those who were left
in office had to learn to speak more respectfully of African
Americans, even if they didn't feel that respect.

Political changes occurred on a federal level as well for African Americans. John Lewis, the former chairman of SNCC, was elected to Congress. Thurgood Marshall became the first black judge to be appointed to the Supreme Court. Robert Weaver became the first black cabinet member, serving as secretary of the Department of Housing and Urban Development. Andrew Young, one of Martin Luther King, Jr.'s aides, was appointed ambassador to the United Nations and later elected mayor of Atlanta, Georgia. By 1984, there were 255 African-American mayors in the United States.

A black mayor and a mostly black board of education were eventually elected in Lowndes County, where Carmichael started the Lowndes County Freedom Organization. In Marion, Selma, and Montgomery, Alabama, where SNCC worked to register black voters during Freedom Summer, blacks finally gained control of the city council and the board of education.

In 1989, the citizens of Jackson, Mississippi, voted in their first black mayor. However, in 1989, Ture still felt that African Americans were a long way from being organized. "In 1965, there were no African mayors in the U.S.A. In 1988, there are 303, all of them except one Republican are loyal Democrats. All of them singularly and in block are powerless inside the racist political structure of the U.S.A." according to Ture. "These African mayors represent the biggest cities in the U.S.A., Detroit, Chicago, Newark, D.C., Atlanta, etc., yet the conditions of the masses of our people are worse today in these very cities than before the advent of African mayors."

Leading SNCC was one of the ways in which Kwame Ture tried to bring about change for African Americans. He took a militant stand and demanded for African Americans the rights enjoyed by other Americans. But because he was so militant, he and his family were followed by the FBI, his passport was taken away, and he was banned from countries connected with Great Britain. In addition to wanting to live in Africa, he felt he had to leave the United States for his safety and peace of mind.

In 1990, Kwame Ture was still living in Conakry, Guinea.

He visits the United States several times a year. He has taught at the university in Conakry. Even now, the FBI continues to watch Ture and his family. He has continued to organize young people of African descent into one worldwide group. He gives speeches throughout the world and sets up work-study programs. In these programs, young people learn about Pan-Africanism and their African heritage.

Both President Sékou Touré and Dr. Kwame Nkrumah died, and Kwame Ture was arrested several times after the death of President Touré in 1984. The reasons for the arrests were mysterious. Some people felt that the military government in Guinea saw Kwame Ture as a threat because he always spoke his mind. This government became stricter than it had been. People were not allowed to speak their minds, and some were punished for not agreeing with the government.

From the "little man" of Trinidad to the black power militant of the United States, to the "Great Man" of Africa, Ture had searched for and found his own truth along the path of struggle. Many people who were active during the 1960s are no longer involved. For Kwame Ture, however, the struggle has never ended. He has continued to fight for the freedom of African people anywhere and everywhere in the world.

> If you're talking about revolution, you had better get hip to studying. If you're not studying, you're doing nothing but fooling yourself. If you are a revolutionary today in the black community you must know Marx, you must know Lenin, you must know Malcolm X, Ché, Fidel, Sékou Touré, Ho Chi Minh, you must know DuBois, you must know Nkrumah, you must know Lumumba, you must know Huey P. Newton, you must know Amiri Baraka [Leroi Jones], Robert Williams, you must know Fannie Lou Hamer, you must know a whole lot of people, a whole lot. Their ideas and their ideologies. Aside from that you must know what is going on in the world at the same time. . . .
>
> -Stokely Carmichael/Kwame Ture

Timetable of Events
in the Life of
Stokely Carmichael

July 29, 1941	Born in Port of Spain, Trinidad
1952	Moves to New York City
1960	Enters Howard University
	Joins Student Nonviolent Coordinating Committee (SNCC) and Nonviolent Action Group (NAG)
1961	Jailed for 53 days for demonstrating
1964	Becomes SNCC director of the second Congressional District in Mississippi
1966	Establishes Lowndes County Freedom Organization
	Becomes chairperson of SNCC
	Makes slogan "Black Power" famous at the Meredith march in Mississippi
1967	Becomes honorary prime minister for the Black Panther Party for Self-Defense
1968	Fired from SNCC
	Marries Miriam Makeba
1969	Establishes All African Peoples Revolutionary Party
	Moves to Guinea
	Resigns from Black Panther Party
1970	Returns to the United States
1971	Receives honorary doctorate of law degree from Shaw University in North Carolina
	Writes *Stokely Speaks: Black Power Back to Pan-Africanism*
1978	Divorced from Miriam Makeba
	Marries Malyatou; they have a son, Bokar Biro
1990	Continues to organize for the AAPRP

SUGGESTED READING

Branch, Taylor. *Parting the Waters: America in the King Years 1954–63*. New York: Simon and Schuster, 1984.

Breitman, George. *Malcolm X Speaks*. New York: Grove Press, 1966.

Carmichael, Stokely. *Stokley Speaks: Black Power Back to Pan-Africanism*. New York: Random House, 1971.

Carmichael, Stokely, and Charles V. Hamilton. *Black Power, Politics of Liberation in America*. New York: Random House, 1967.

*Du Bois, W. E. B. *The Souls of Black Folk*. New York: Dodd, 1979.

Morris, Aldon. *The Origins of the Civil Rights Movement*. New York: The Free Press, 1984.

*Robinson, Dorothy. *The Legend of Africania*. Chicago: Johnson, 1974.

*Santrey, Laurence. *Young Frederick Douglass: Fight for Freedom*. New York: Troll, 1983.

Ture, Kwame. "For the African Revolution." *Voices of the African Revolution No. 1*. London Pan-African Association, 1987.

*Wayne, Bennett, ed. *Black Crusaders for Freedom*. New York: Garrard, 1974.

Williams, Juan. *Eyes on the Prize*. New York: Viking, 1987.

*Readers of *Stokely Carmichael: The Story of Black Power* will find these books particularly readable.

SOURCES

Anthony, Earl. *Picking up the Gun*. New York: Pyramid Books/Dial, 1971.

Blumberg, Rhoda Lois. *Civil Rights: The 1960s Freedom Struggle*. Boston: Twayne, 1984.

Breitman, George. *Malcolm X Speaks*. New York: Grove Press, 1966.

Carmichael, Stokely. *Stokely Speaks, Black Power to Pan-Africanism*. New York: Random House, 1971.

Carmichael, Stokely, and Charles V. Hamilton. *Black Power, Politics of Liberation in America*. New York: Random House, 1967.

Carson, Clayborne. *In Struggle, SNCC and the Black Awakening of the 1960s*. Cambridge, MA: Harvard University Press, 1981.

Civil Rights Leaders in Profile. New York: Facts on File, 1979.

Fairclough, Adam. *To Redeem the Soul of America: The Southern Christian Leadership Conference and Martin Luther King, Jr.* Athens, GA: The University of Georgia Press, 1987.

Foner, Philip S. *Voice of Black America*. New York: Simon and Schuster, 1972

Forman, James. *The Making of a Black Revolutionary*. Seattle, WA: Open Hand Press, 1987.

Friedman, Leon ed. *The Civil Rights Reader: Basic Documents of the Civil Rights Movement*. New York: Walker, 1968.

Grant, Joann. *Black Protest, History, Document, and Analyses*. New York: Fawcett, 1968.

Killens, John O. *Black Man's Burden*. New York: Pocket Books, 1969.

King, Mary. *Freedom Song: A Personal Story of the 1960s Civil Rights Movement*. New York: Morrow, 1987.

Link, Arthur S., and William B. Catton. *American Epoch*. New York: Knopf, 1965.

Makeba, Miriam. *Makeba*. New York: New American Library, 1988.

Martin, Tony. *The Pan-African Connection*. Wellesley, MA: The Majority Press, 1983.

Meier, August, and Elliott Rudwick. *Black Protest in the Sixties*. Chicago: New York Times/Quadrangle, 1970.

Raines, Howell. *My Soul Is Rested: The Story of the Civil Rights Movement in the Deep South*. New York: Penguin, 1983.

Thirty Years of African Liberation Day. All African People's Revolutionary Party pamphlet, May 25, 1988.

Ture, Kwame. "For the African Revolution." *Voices of the African Revolution No. 1*. London Pan-African Association, January, 1987.

Wagstaff, Thomas. *Black Power: The Radical Response to White America*. Mission Hills: Glencoe Press, 1969.

Williams, Juan. *Eyes on the Prize*. New York: Viking, 1987.

Zinn, Howard. *The New Abolitionists*. New York: Beacon Press, 1965.

INTERVIEWS

The Reverend James Anderson, June 1989, Selma, Alabama.

David Brother, September 1989, New York City.

Elaine Carmichael, September 1989, Trinidad.

Mabel Carmichael, September 1989, New York City.

F.D. Reese, June 1989, Selma, Alabama.

Albert Turner, June 1989, Marion, Alabama.

INDEX

About the Author

Jacqueline Johnson is a free-lance writer living in New York. She is the winner of the 1987 Middle Atlantic Writers Association Creative Writing Award in Poetry. A member of the New Renaissance Writers Guild, the John O. Killins Writers Workshop, and the Harlem Writers Guild, Ms. Johnson is currently a 1989 Gregory Millard Fellow of the New York Foundation for the Arts Award in Poetry.

Text permissions:

From *Black Power: The Politics of Liberation in America* by Stokely Carmichael and Charles V. Hamilton. Copyright © 1967 by Stokely Carmichael and Charles Hamilton. Reprinted by permission of Random House, Inc.

From *Stokely Speaks* by Stokely Carmichael. Copyright © 1965, 1971 by Stokely Carmichael. Reprinted by permission of Random House, Inc.

From *We Shall Overcome: Songs of the Southern Freedom Movement*, compiled and edited by Guy and Candie Carawan. Copyright © 1963 Oak Publications. All rights reserved. Reprinted by permission.

From *The Voice of Black America* by Philip S. Foner. Copyright © 1972. Reprinted by permission of Simon & Schuster, Inc.

From "From My People" from *This Is My Century: New and Collected Poems* by Margaret Walker. Copyright © 1989 by Margaret Walker Alexander. Reprinted by permission of the University of Georgia Press.

From "Say It Loud, I'm Black and I'm Proud" by James Brown. Copyright © 1968 by Golo Publishing Co. All rights administered by Chappell & Co. All rights reserved. Used by permission.

From the film series *Eyes on the Prize: America's Civil Rights Years, 1954–1965*. Copyright © 1987 by Blackside, Inc. All rights Reserved. Reprinted by Permission.

From *Eyes on the Prize: America's Civil Rights Years, 1954-1965* by Juan Williams and the Eyes On The Prize production team. Published by Viking Penguin. Copyright © 1987 by Blackside, Inc. Reprinted with permission of Blackside, Inc.

First appeared in *Esquire*, "Brilliancy of Black," January 1967, by Bernard Weinraub. Reprinted courtesy of the Hearst Corporation, 1990.

From *Black Man's Burden* by John Oliver Killens. Copyright © 1965 by John Oliver Killens. Reprinted by permission of International Creative Management, Inc.

The quotations from Malcolm X on pp. 76 and 97 are taken from pp. 116 and 129, respectively, of *Malcolm X Speaks* (copyright © 1965 by Betty Shabazz and Pathfinder Press), and are reproduced by permission of Pathfinder Press.

Picture Credits: AP/Wide World Photos: 26, 42, 65, 94, 99, 101, 103, 112, 120; Carmichael family: 12; Moorland-Spingarn Research Center: 115; Sam Falk/NYT Pictures: 102; George Tames/NYT Pictures: 56; Schomburg Center for Research in Black Culture, N.Y. Public Library, Astor, Lenox and Tilden Foundations: cover portrait (Lynn B. Padwe), 9, 68, 80, 92 (Laurance Henry Collection); UPI/Bettman: cover background, 79, 104.